Family Dynamics and Intergenerational Relations

About the Authors

Sunil K. Verma is working as Assistant Professor in Vivekananda College, Delhi University. He has published more than 20 research papers in and reputed nationals and international journals in the area of Gerontology and Applied Social Psychology and participated various National and International Conferences. He has been involved in various research projects, some of which are results of multinational collaborations. Dr. Verma has been recognized as "Emerging Psychologist" by the organizers of International Congress of Psychology 2012 in Cape Town and has received several Fellowships to participate in International Conferences from UGC, IUPSY and ARTS.

Atluri Satyanarayana, Former Professor and Head of Sociology at University of Allahabad. His major interests are in the areas of agrarian development, peasant movements, farmer's suicide, intergenerational relation and child labour. He had intensively published in this area. He has also brought two books on Technology Work and Social Relations in Agriculture and Changing Village India. Apart from this he completed a research project on Contemporary Peasant Movements in Democratic Society: Case of BKU and carried Restudy of Jhabiran Village. He was also convenor of RC 17 in Indian Sociological Association.

FAMILY DYNAMICS AND INTERGENERATIONAL RELATIONS

A Psycho-Social Analysis

Sunil K. Verma
A. Satyanarayana

CONCEPT PUBLISHING COMPANY PVT. LTD.
NEW DELHI-110059

ISBN-13: 978-93-86682-45-1

First Published 2018

Published and Printed by

Concept Since 1974

Concept Publishing Company Pvt. Ltd.
A/15-16, Commercial Block, Mohan Garden,
New Delhi-110059 (INDIA)
T: 91 11 25351460, 91 11 25351794
E: publishing@conceptpub.com; *W*: www.conceptpub.com

Cataloging in Publication Data--Courtesy: D.K. Agencies (P) Ltd. <docinfo@dkagencies.com>

Verma, Sunil K., author.
Family dynamics and intergenerational relations : a psycho-social analysis / Sunil K. Verma, A. Satyanarayana.
pages cm
Includes bibliographical references and index.
ISBN 9789386682451

1. Intergenerational relations—India. 2. Families—India. 3. Families—India—Psychological aspects. I. Satyanarayana, A. (Atluri), author. II. Title.

LCC HM726.V47 2018 DDC 306.8740954 23

Foreword

A family is a primary social institution which connects between generations and forms the most important social bonds in all societies. With the rise of industrialization and mechanization of agriculture, the system of large family, where three to four generations lived together has been changing to the nuclear family of two generations consisting of parents and their children. A family provides social, emotional, economic security and functions as the first educational institution to socialize the younger generation by transforming them to be effective in their socio-cultural milieu. The older generation also transfers to the younger generation socio-cultural practices with the objective to maintain continuity. Over time norms and patterns have evolved in all cultures with variations providing stability to the functioning of respective societies for intergenerational living arrangements, obligations, support, inheritance, and relationships. Family inculcates in us, to respect, to take responsibility, to reciprocate, and to tolerate which all together provide resilience and stability to the intergenerational relationship. Honesty is the key tool to help parenting and grandparenting and two or more adult generations keep evolving new ways of relating and interacting.

The recent decades have been going through unprecedented widespread technological changes with economic development influencing societal and cultural institutions and practices affecting intergenerational relationships in today's families. The intergenerational relationship which "stood the test of time" is facing challenges of extraordinary nature. The problem is much more complex in India as we continue to be both rural and urban;

modern and traditional; industrial and agricultural; organized and unorganized economy; as well as having both nuclear and joint families. In this context, this book *"Family Dynamics and Intergenerational Relations: A Psycho-Social Analysis"* authored by Dr. Sunil K. Verma and Dr. A. Satyanarayana is a welcome publication. It presents interdisciplinary perspectives for understanding intergenerational relations in a family in varied socio-cultural economic contexts. Based on extensive empirical study Dr. Verma and Dr. Satyanarayana have competently answered the questions related to the way priority of values, of father-son, mother-in-law, daughter-in-laws in the family and other socio-psychological factors determine the pattern of their intergenerational relationship and the way such relationship affect their well-being. I am sure that psychologists and sociologists and general readers would find it interesting reading and would be benefited in terms of their understanding of the subject.

28 February, 2018

Professor Janak Pandey
ICSSR National Fellow and
Founder Vice Chancellor,
Central University of Bihar
Bihar

Preface

My academic journey began in this topic when I was carrying out a dissertation for the partial fulfilment of requirements of Master of Art in Psychology which focused on a comparative study on working and non-working rural and urban elderly and their quality of life. After completing my masters, I enrolled into D. Phil. Programme at the Department of Psychology, University of Allahabad. The focus of my work was on the experience of elderly who are living in an old age home and those living with family. During the pilot fieldwork, I found that the major problem experienced by elderly was that of support and care from family members as well as the issue of dissimilarities in ideas and values. So, I shifted my interest and started working on issues of intergenerational relations.

My interest in the field of gerontology was fuelled by my past when I was a child who belonged to a joint family with over ten members. I always used to wonder what it would be like for the elderly persons who are abandoned by their families or those living in old age homes. I believed that old age homes were the worst place to be, till the time my belief was challenged by my neighbours who treated their aging father with disdain and disregard. Thus, I began my work in the field of aging and intergenerational relationships along with Satyanarayana (the co-author and my mentor). We discussed on the various aspects of family dynamics and social gerontology, and since we both came from different academic backgrounds (with Satyanarayana belonging to the discipline of Sociology and having mastery in qualitative methods, whereas Sunil having master's degree in Applied Social Psychology and having knowledge of quantitative methods) we brought in diverse perspectives. Our common ground was the shared interest to identify the social issues and process which affect or facilitate the intergenerational relations in Indian cultural context. Thus, we have adopted an interdisciplinary lens to study the phenomena which has enriched our work.

Intergenerational relationships have mostly been studied from the old age perspectives. The voice of the youth has somehow been sidelined in this important area of study. Also, the import of social psychological elements to understand the dynamics of intergenerational relationships is little. In my work, I have tried to focus on all relationships that are involved in the power tussle. It is intriguing to study power dynamics that not only emanates from the authority (that further comes from hierarchy and power structures) in a family, but also the fluid nature of such hierarchy which changes depending upon a host of social psychological and sociological factors. The wise aged patriarchy in a rural family has different degree of control over family decision-making in contrast to that of a retired elderly residing in an urban society. This book tries to understand the process of various forms of intergenerational relationships (conflict, solidarity, and ambivalence) in reference to Robert & Bengtson (1991) solidarity model with the modification and addition of some other variables to suit the Indian cultural context. This book also discusses the effect of demographic changes in terms of socio-economic class and rural and urban location on the experience of intergenerational relationships. Apart from these aspects, this book also emphasizes on cross-generational comparison regarding experience of well-being in reference to intergenerational relationship.

We hope that this book with its cultural treatment to the topic will be a useful resource for educators and academicians, researchers and students working in the area of family dynamics, intergenerational relations and social gerontology.

29th March, 2018

Sunil K. Verma
and
A. Satyanarayana

Acknowledgements

This book is a love of labour and an in-depth research work, which would not have been possible without the support and guidance of my teachers and friends. It has been the result of the constant encouragement and guidance by Prof. Janak Pandey, Central University of Bihar, Bihar and Prof. Girishwar Misra, Mahatma Gandhi International Hindi University at Wardha, Maharashtra. It is their conviction and faith in me that has constantly inspired me to understand and successfully complete the task. I express my deepest gratitude to both my Gurus. I am thankful to my friends Pankaj, Sujeet, Shivantika, Dharmendra, Rishabh, Tushar, Ashish and Satyabrat who took time to review this book and provide their invaluable suggestions and inputs.

I would also like to thank my colleagues from Department of Applied Psychology, Vivekananda College, University of Delhi, Delhi for their unwavering support. My family has always trusted my abilities, provided me with emotional support and has stimulated my academic pursuits.

I would like to reiterate my thanks to my students Sweta, Divya and Soorya who assisted me in all the work whenever I needed their support.

I also express my gratitude to the Divine for His infinite blessings.

Sunil K. Verma
and
A. Satyanarayana

Contents

List of Tables and Figures

TABLES

FIGURES

Introduction

Intergenerational relations deal with the interaction between two or more generations, which can be between parents and children, grandparents and grandchildren, or between any old and young person in family or otherwise. Intergenerational relations in family share kinship activities, having frequent contact with each other and engaging in a network of mutual assistance both within and between generations (Hill, Foote, Aldous, Carlson & MacDonald, 1970). In the present time, the phenomenon of intergenerational relations is a concern in both developing as well as in developed countries.

Aging emerged as a new social concern with the demographic transition of the population and changing value orientations of younger generation towards their older generation. This led to the emergence of Gerontology as a separate discipline. Social scientists and reformers showed greater interest in the phenomena of intergenerational relations during the period of Industrial Revolution in the United States (Manheim, 1952; Eisenstadt, 1956; Slater, 1979). The industrial revolution and technological changes have resulted in differentiation of roles within the family that contribute to individualism and loss of status, power, and authority of the elderly. Early studies on intergenerational relations have emphasized extensively on the generation gap, generation conflict, generational solidarity, and generational ambivalence. In general, the field of intergenerational relations has focused its research towards treatment meted out to elderly and problems they face due to social change.

In 1971, Durganand Sinha wrote a book *"Mughal Syndrome"* based on his study of the generation gap in India, which provided a perspective to the reader to see how the Mughal Empire replaced older generation and how power and authority were captured by the younger generation. Other studies in this area have emphasized on increasing generation gap, discrepancy in the values and attitude between older and younger generation, the impact of social change on intergenerational relations and how the elderly status are affected by this change (Gangrade, 1975; Mishra and Prasad, 1978; Tiwari and Mishra, 1979; Mishra, 2004; Batra and Bhaumik, 2004). Besides scholarly works, intergenerational issues have attracted the attention of film-makers also. For example, the movie *Mughal-e-Azam* released in 1960 depicts the story of relational dynamics between Mughal Emperor Akbar and his son Jahangir. The film focuses on how father and son differ in terms of values and norms of behaviour, leading to war like situation between them. Another movie *Avtaar* (1983) focuses on how the younger generation is self-oriented and selfish, ignore their elderly parents, bring separation between their parents, and make their parents feel helpless, isolated, and alienated. From mid-1990 to 2008, a series of movies such as "*Rishta a Love Bond*", "*Waqt*" and "*Baghban*" captured the theme of generational differences between older and younger generation.

As a Social scientist, my primary question is whether only negativity characterizes relationships between generations or is there any possibility of positivity? Indian research on generational relations has sparsely considered the life of Rama or Shrawan Kumar from the great Indian epic *Ramayana* to understand the process of intergenerational relations. Overall, in literature, the term generation has been used with a negative connotation, and this is primarily the case with the developed world. In the developing world especially India, the word generation is used with a positive connotation that forms an integral part of joint family system pervading the Indian society. Put differently, in an Indian family, the generational formula is frequently used to understand the function of a joint family system. Joint family is to be distinguished from the coparcenary. The word 'coparcenary' comprises of those who by birth take an interest in the joint or coparcenary property, i.e. a person himself, his sons, sons' son and sons' grandson: there is four generation of males. It refers to the transfer of power and property from older generation to younger generation. If the common male ancestor is included, it is four generations, and if excluded three generations (Shah, 1998: 97).

In India, joint family is one of the most prestigious institutions that have survived through the ages. India has a documented heritage of stable family life and structure which has been able to withstand the vicissitudes over the centuries (Sinha, 1984). Indian family, like most families in Oriental cultures, is considered strong, well knit, resilient, and enduring. Simultaneously, heterogeneity and diversity also characterize the family life in India. In the joint family system, two or three generations live together with differentiated roles and responsibilities. For example, father is perceived as the breadwinner while a mother is responsible for the upbringing of children, taking care of their needs, providing love, care, and protection. Grandfathers play the role of the custodian of the culture and conventions of the family, and take care of grandchildren in the absence of their parents and socialize with them. As the reciprocity norm indicates, parents in the family are expected to respect their elders, provide care to younger ones, and extend help at home whenever necessary. These relations are hierarchical in nature (Pandey, 2007). In sum; the generations have emotional as well as materialistic interdependency between them. Despite generational differences in values and attitude, they share emotional bonding and use various types of psycho-social strategies to maintain intergenerational relationships.

The Scheme of Chapterization

The book has been broadly divided into eight chapters.

Chapter 1: **Journey of Intergenerational Relations Research: Issues and Debates:** This review chapter comprehensively covers all aspects of intergenerational relations after 1942 to 2012 and provides a critical analysis.

Chapter 2: **Method and Methodologies in Intergenerational Relations:** This chapter covers the methodological issues in intergenerational research along with a description of the methods used to study the phenomena, a combination of methods approach and its merit and demerits, sample and field description.

Chapter 3: **Pattern of Intergenerational Relations in Indian Family:** This chapter deals with the model of intergenerational relations and determining factor with demographic variations and causes behind it.

Chapter 4: **Family Dynamics and Psycho-Social Process of Intergenerational Solidarity:** This chapter explains the process of intergenerational solidarity with the help of family interaction process and also explicates the techniques people use to maintain the solidarity.

Chapter 5: **Family Functioning and Process of Intergenerational Ambivalences:** In this chapter, the process of intergenerational ambivalence is explained with the help of family interaction process, and the techniques people used to maintain the ambivalence are also discussed.

Chapter 6: **Family Dynamics and Process of Intergenerational Conflict:** This chapter explains the process of intergenerational conflict with the family interaction process, and what are outlines of the techniques people used to minimize the conflict.

Chapter 7: **Intergenerational Relations and Well-being:** This chapter deals with the Psycho-Social consequences of intergenerational relations and role demographic variable in these experiences.

Chapter 8: **Concluding Remarks and Future Direction of Research:** As per the name this chapter is based on concluding the monograph and suggesting future direction for research.

1
Journey of Intergenerational Research: Issues and Debates

Introduction

Intergenerational researches cover the two major perspectives, i.e. children values, which cover the values of children, offspring socialization and immigrant studies. Beside these, the other perspectives, which are working in the area of Intergenerational Research, i.e. Aging and Social Process. The perspective covers elderly and their family life, old age problem, aging and economy and their psycho-social consequences. In this chapter, Intergenerational research covers the perspective of aging and social process.

Intergenerational relations deal with the *interaction* between *more than two generations,* which can be between parent and children, grandparent and grandchildren, or any old person and young person whether related or not through blood or otherwise. Intergenerational relations in family share kinship activities, characterised by frequent contacts with members of family and show patterns of mutual assistance within and between generations (Hill, Foote, Aldous, Carlson & MacDonald, 1970). The phenomenon of intergenerational relations is a concern in both developing and developed countries in the contemporary period.

Review of literature reveals that prior to 1920s, aging was concerned with the childhood and adolescence, which were viewed as the essential developmental stages in the life cycle. However, *The Second Half of Life* (Hall, 1922) and *Problems of Aging* (Cowdry, 1939) were two exceptions to the above mentioned trends. Though anthropologists have previously documented the status and treatment of the elderly in a number of tribal and agrarian societies, the interest in aging was limited, till Twentieth century, to social welfare programmes and developing social policies which resulted from increased visibility of elderly population regulated in aged centric welfare policies like income maintenance, employment and social welfare (Epstein, 1922).

In early 1940s, social scientists' attention was diverted on the social significance of old age, attitudes and adjustment to old age (Landis, 1940), adjustment to age and gender roles (Cottrell, 1942), age and gender in the social structure (Parsons, 1942), formation and function of age based norms (Linton, 1942). They categorized aging as chronological, biological, psychological and social. Social Scientists and gerontologists, in generational analysis, were mainly concerned with the effect of emerging age groups either in maintenance of social order or discontinuity (conflict) in the existing social order. Besides, they are concerned with the impact of collective action of a particular age group on social, economic and political aspects of life.

Mannheim (1952) was probably the first to see that generational relations were comprehended through the concept of "generational problem". Eisenstadts (1956) was concerned with the following questions: (a) how intergenerational interactions affect continuity and change in the social order; (b) within generation how age strata are differentiated; (c) how generations are differentiated; (d) how generation moves from one age grade to another and what patterns of relations develop between generations, particularly between younger and older members of society? According to him, age as a heterogeneous group is prevalent in societies where age, gender, kinship are the basic units in the division of labour. In industrial societies, patterns of interactions become segmented according to common age-related interests and needs and homogenous age group are observed. Bengtson *et al.* (1974) explained five issues, which are important in the comprehension of generational relations. They are:

- definition and dimensions of generation as a construct (Social construction);
- assessment of the continuity and discontinuity between generations;

- exploration of the continuity of generational unit over a time period; and
- analysis of solidarity within cohort/generation and finally articulation between generations and other dimensions of social structure.

The intergenerational relations in complex societies are greatly affected by the interaction of technological development with division of labour. For instance, the development of formalized youth groups will be more, if social institutions are made unavailable to younger generations. Besides this, the family fails to socialize the young to participate in the specialized roles in the society. A Generation is also considered a constant dynamic factor that may results in social change. The older generations cease to exist, taking with them certain cultural perspectives, while the new generation emerges and undertakes a new journey with the imparted accumulated culture and develop it further by selecting some elements from it, and by using it in different ways.

The functionalist perspective suggests that intergenerational conflict, to some extent, can also result from the differences in the personalities of members of different generations as well as the difference in power and status associated with the members of different generations within the social system. Mannheim (1972) also pointed out that people belonging to different generations are at different stages of socialization, i.e. early socialization and late socialization (Inkles) and were born in different historical periods. These two factors affect the development of differences in age based personalities. Such differences are manifested occasionally in conflict between parent and children. The intensity of overt conflict between generations is related to the degree of social change, complexity and integration (Davis, 1942).

Slater (1970) explored the socialization processes within the contemporary family settings and suggests that rebellion is not the main culprit in intergenerational conflict but surprisingly its conformity. The arrangement is such that in contemporary family, more conformity between generations was observed as the children adopted the values of their parents during the socialization process. The children and youth in the modern society have adopted values that are far from moral integrity and make little sense in terms of the needs of self given demands of the post-industrial culture.

The key component of generational analysis is intergenerational continuity and discontinuity and intergenerational transmission of behaviour and the review of studies in intergenerational relations also reveal the existence of intergenerational similarities between the elder and the younger (Aldous & Hill, 1965; Kensiston, 1968; Jennings & Niemi, 1968; Troll *et al.*, 1969; Hill, 1970; Thomas, 1971; Kendel & Lesser, 1972; Rieley *et al.*, 1972). It also reveals three types of trend, i.e.

- Continuity of cultural values between generations;
- Emergence of counter-culture; and
- All the differences share age-based differences on attitude and values.

Altbach and Peterson (1972) studied generational differences as a matter of political affiliation and ideology and found that it resulted in student movement of youth and radical movement of adults. The student movements in 1960s were a consonance of wide-spread experimentation with deviant life style in terms of their preference for cloth, music and dance and liberalized social and sexual norms. It leads to the development of counter-culture or countra-culture (Orum, 1972). The youth counter-culture of sixties had values such as love, peace, freedom, cooperation, sharing, egalitarianism, honesty and openness, self-expression, naturalness humanism, pleasure, spontaneity and romantic mysticism (Flack, 1967; Pitts, 1969; Slater, 1970; Berger, 1971; Davis, 1971; Brown, 1973; Wieder & Zimmerman, 1974). These students belonged disproportionately to upper middle class urban families to parents who were professionals. These parents promoted values of secularism, liberalism, egalitarianism, and humanitarianism and also encouraged autonomy and self-expression in their children, which promoted the counter-culture in mid-sixties in the U.S. (Salomon, 1964; Westby & Braungart, 1966; Flacks, 1967).

Bengtson and Black (1973) suggested a social change model for the analysis of "generational relations" in generational cycle. According to this model the change (a) fosters the emergence of new values; (b) specific alternative ideal pattern of behaviour aimed at actualizing these values; (c) attempts to actualize these alternatives by testing them out in their everyday lives; and (d) selecting among one or more of the alternative patterns which depart the least from the established ways of behaving can be met with the least resistance from older generation and, thus, maybe, incorporated into conventional life styles, producing less dramatic change. The more radical alternatives may require special condition if they are to be experimented with, *e.g.* the certain communes or segregated youth communities.

Keeping in view the absence of scholarly attention to study intergenerational studies relating to value orientations, the attention of scholars shifted to survey research findings of which forced Yankelovich (1970) to think again his earlier view hold that there exists very little differences in the attitudes and values between generations. He conducted successive interviews on college students during 1968-1971 and found that there are shifts in values and attitudes across generations.

Slater (1970) observed the development of a new culture among youth that was different from the old generation and such cultural differences were assumed as the consequence orientation of man towards nature. For instance, if their old generation perceives that the resources are scarce while the youth perceives recourses to be in abundance, than the differential perception of resources will be one of the basis of the development of intergenerational cultural differences. Thomas (1974) tried to understand generational differences in various belief levels and found that intermediate level of beliefs related to authority show greater generational discontinuity, especially in context to the authenticity of national institutions. The period of 60s marked the convergence of distractive generational ideology among the substantial segments of American youth. Starr (1974) tried to understand the attitude towards violence and sex in college youth and found that peace and love among generations were deeply entrenched in the structural changes due to the advanced industrial development. Political and economic forces hostile to their thrust could represent the most visible manifestation of this new ideology. However, the impulses that found expression in the ideology of the peace and love generation have been without effect. Intergenerational factors influence level of intergenerational influences (for instance drug use; Kandel, 1974). Berger & Hacket (1974) studied rural hippie communes and suggested that "a clear attenuation of the normative differences usually ascribe to children on the ground of their age. The participation of children in drug use and the sex as well as their autonomy in the settlement of their disputes, are cited as examples for this decline in age grading. Interpretation is offered in the ways in which this equalitarian conception of children is systematically sustained by other facts of communal life and by the ideological posture of parents. Finally, inference is drawn from the decline of age grading in the communes of the counter-culture of possible changes in the relation between the generations in the future."

Kasschau (1974) tried to explore youth conscious development in four groups of youth—white collar and blue collar and students and non-students. The research employed a social movement perspective and assumed that there would be a developmental sequence between initial awareness to crystallize ideology and in the form of collective action to behaviour expression. He found important subtleties in the spread of generational consciousness and the youth movement to the blue collar and non-student segments of the youth population. These findings suggest that the generational analysis must consider two sets of time related conditions: (a) some historical events that occur with the passage of time, which may be decisively relevant in the shaping of generational unit; (b) the developmental events that occur in the lives of individuals as they grow old (Bengston, 1973); and (c) they are related to the succession of cohorts as one age stratum replaces their other lower positions of power and responsibilities (Ryder,1965; Riley, Johnson & Foner, 1972).

Ragan and Dowd (1974) argued that generational analysis tends to focus on youth movements and ideologies, in keeping with the Mannheim's emphasis on new generations. The generational aspects of a political movement among the older generations also warrants the possibility of the emergence of that political consciousness and racial movements of the aged be discussed with the emphasis on political expression in the current generation of older people.

Intergenerational relations can also be understood within an association, for example families, political parties, and professional groups.

Intergenerational Relations in Family

Family is a primary social group providing an environment for the care of children. It also renders affection and social bonding throughout the life cycle for emotional, social, economic, and health support in old age. It is the first school for socialization for children and transmission of values from older to younger generation. The structure of family influences the interaction pattern within and between generations. Most of the families are made up of two (parents-children) or three (grandparents, parents and children) generations. As the life expectancy is increasing the four-generation family (great grandparents, grandparents, parents and children) is also becoming a reality. Thus, the concept generation refers to the ranked descent within the extended family system (Troll, 1970; Bengtson, 1975; Troll & Bengtson, 1979). This ranking is related to chronological age. Role allocation within the biological family unit is based on birth order, marital status, and the procreation pattern of succeeding generations. Thus power, authority, and prestige within the extended kinship system are primarily based on ascription, and achievement based inequalities are more pronounced in the larger society.

Intergenerational interactions can be comprehended at micro-level, i.e. within a family and also at macro-level, i.e. the broader society. For example, aggregates of the grandparents, parents and children may interact on the societal level as a member of particular generation or generational unit. They will be exposed to particular societal process (discrimination, stratification, socialization and conflict). At the same time, as a member of extended kinship system with varying degree of filial bonding, they interact with not only other generations within the family but also with the age cohort in the kinship system. The socialization and social control process within the dual structure can create conflict and confusion, especially with respect to the transmission of values and other cultural characteristics from one generation to the next. The competing prestige of both the parents and the peer group, seeks to impose values and behaviours that can create role conflict for the adolescents, social conflict and change in the society.

Review of Intergenerational Relations with family reveals three patterns of Intergenerational relations, i.e. conflict, solidarity and ambivalence.

Inter-Generational Conflict

Differences on matters of values, needs and life styles are observed between generations and such differences lead to conflicts between generations. This can be termed as an intergenerational conflict. If conflict arises within the family, it is more likely to occur between parent and children during the critical years of identity formation and independent assertion.

Sometimes intergenerational conflicts may result in the formation of age homogeneous political or social groups at macro-level seeking change or stability in society.

Cohen and Ganes (1978) argued that socialization involves two-way process of interaction, negotiation and interpretation of meanings. On the basis of negotiation and meanings, either cohesiveness or conflict between generations will emerge within families. Bengtson & Keeupers (1970) found that older generation has an interest in the *status quo* and in the maintenance and continuity of those values that were considered as salience to them. Therefore, they seek to inculcate similar values in younger generation. Younger people seek to develop a life style and unique set of values that are different from the older generation and promote differences between the generations. Such intergenerational differences in values and life style may be perceived as a source of intergenerational conflict.

Fengler and Wood (1972) studied value differences in families continuing three generation-controlling variables like gender, education, religion and place of residence. They found that age difference resulted in generational differences in values and attitudes. Laufer & Bengtson (1974) disagreed with the age based differences on similarity or intergenerational differences.

Stenman (1979) examined the parent and child conflict during adulthood in the U.S. in three generational families. He suggested that crisis in the family like illness, death of one parent, financial difficulties for the elderly person, or a divorce or financial crisis on the part of the offspring can increase parent child dependency during middle adulthood. These crises can result in three types of the intergenerational conflicts in the family:

1. *Continuing Conflict*: The underlying tension of the crisis in the middle adulthood will always exists in relation to meaning of life, values morals, friends or religion;

2. *New Conflicts*: In this parents and adult children disagree on their respective roles of caring the surviving parents or rising the third generation; and
3. *Unresolved Conflict*: In childhood, conflict may reappear with renewed or increased interaction between parents and adult child.

In aging society, the aged members will experience a loss of political power as this power will shift towards older adults, due to their considerable and still progressing as their voting power that would make them appealing to politicians and power brokers. This can prove as a significant reason for open conflict between younger and older generations more than covert prejudice or stereotypes against elderly (Butler, 1969). Older adults have more time at their perusal thus making them more capable of affecting the local or Central Government through political mobilization. The number of older adults and children combined dependent on the work force may not experience a greater growth as there will be older adults owning control on greater share of resources. In sum, there is a greater possibility of intergenerational conflict at stake are power, financial resources, justice and social identity aspiration leading to intergenerational conflict (Simmel,1950; Sherif & Sherief,1953; Austin,1979; Tajfel & Turner,1979). On the basis of these studies four sources of intergenerational conflict, i.e. power, resources, justice and social identity are observed.

There is a greater increase in intergenerational conflict between parents and children at the advent of adolescence and is usually at its peak. However, it gradually declines by late adolescence and young adulthood. This variation can be attributed to the establishment of greater autonomy and independence, development of own personal identities, adoption of value system and fostering social relationships with individuals other than parents. The transition from family home to college may lead to loosening of parental control and can contribute to the decrease in family conflict (Arnett,1999; Laursen, Coy & Collins, 1998). Laursen *et al.* (1998) argued that the majority of empirical researches on intergenerational relations in family were conducted mostly on European and American population, neglecting the role of cultural factors in the development of intergenerational conflicts and their management.

Sluzki (1979) and Uba (1994) argued that theories and research on Asian American immigrant families surprisingly present a different developmental pattern for intergenerational conflicts. Particularly, the Asian immigrants' parents acknowledge the conflicting cultural demands their children have to deal with and thus, allow their children to progress in their own way and develop their own courses of life. At the same time, many Asian immigrant parents also seek to make their children remain connected to their roots by making efforts to socialize them to espouse the values and traditions of their home culture through cultural specific parenting techniques (Chao, 2000). The U.S. raised Asian children experience difficulties in balancing these family values and expectations with mainstream western values and life style (Fuligni, Tseng & Lam, 1999). Thus, acculturation-enculturation increases the frequency of intergenerational family conflicts between Asian immigrants parents and children rooted in the U.S., particularly when disagreement occurs with regards of acting in accordance to family values, expectations and traditions (Gimchung, 2001; Lee *et al.*, 2000; Phinney Ong & Madden, 2000; Ying Lee, Tsai Lee & Tsang, 2000). Such intergenerational conflict persists in the late adolescence and young adult hood, (Greeberg & Chean, 1996; Lee *et al.*, 2000; Lee & Liu, 2001). Intergenerational differences in values and rate of acculturation of generation often have an impact on intergenerational conflicts (Ho, 1987; Lin, 1986; Min, 1998) unlike family conflict within European American families (Arneet, 1999; Laursen *et al.*, 1998). Uba (1994) studied Chinese, Vietnamese, American college students and found that the children "recognize the cultural gap between themselves and their family is enhancing every year and resulting in anguish and tension due to the expectations of the parents who believe that their children will give priority to family obligations and duties and they wish their children to seek autonomy at a latter age" (Feldman & Rosenthal, 1990; Fuligni & Padersen, 2002). Ishei & Kuntz (1997) note that the transition to college of Asian American children makes it difficult for their parents to exert control than when their children live at their family home. Even when the children stay at home, the parents find it difficult to supervise their daily activities due to their emerging greater freedom and opportunities independent of family.

Laursen and Collins (1994) reveal that intergenerational conflict in family generally occurs during adolescence over issue of autonomy and independence. The children emphasize on Western individualistic values, attitude, life styles, while the elderly gives priority to collectivistic values. Such differences in value are a source of conflict between generations within family. These cultural differences between parents and children get accentuated when the children join college. It further results in greater misunderstanding and conflict between generations (Lee, Choe, Kim & Nago, 2000). Value contrast (i.e. individualism and collectivism) may result in frequent and distressing conflicts between parents and their young adult children (Zhou & Bankston, 1998).

Children who assert more on their autonomy and independence experience frequent intergenerational conflict in family and less cohesion with their parents (Collins & Russell, 1991; Fuligni, 1998; Green Berg & Chain, 1996; Gold, 1989). Seelbach & Die (1988), in their study found that families in with multiple generations reside under the same roof, is more likely to increase stress and conflict due to the frustration that arises from the situations with parental egocentrism encounters adolescent egocentrism and often results in alienation and segregation. In such situations, despite co-residence, there is little mutual understanding among family members. This further gets intensified in the absence of fluency in a common language, further intensifying alienation and segregation with little hope to counter the ever-widening gulf (Lee & Cynn, 1991).

Angel and Angel (1992) studied a sample of immigrants living in multigenerational households and found that such households reduced loneliness and stress level. But Katz & Lowenstein (1999) indicate that these results are relevant only for the older generation. Padilla, *et al.* (2016) found that (conflict in family relationships predicted increases in parent-youth discrepancies in families values rather than the opposite.)

Inter-Generational Solidarity

Solidarity can be defined as doing something for someone. Intergenerational solidarity based on kinship, has not always been found in modern societies. According to Legors (2002) intergenerational solidarity is referred to positive interactions between generations of grandparents, parents and children that counter-balances the ups and downs of life.

According to Durkhiem (1928), solidarity indicated a form of social integration where complementary or role speculations are fulfilled and where anomic and egoistic tendencies are disapproved by the society. Sociologists today view family solidarity as a fluid concept that might strongly be associated to life course events. It can be asymmetric or balanced and deals with perception of social support, complementary or role speculations based relations among family members and members' kin (Bengtson *et al.*, 2002; Komter & Vellebergh, 2002).

According to Merz (2005), intergenerational solidarity refers to processes within intimate interpersonal relationship, mostly occurring within families. The common family provides these relationships with an exclusive and irreversible quality.

The research evidence for the existence of some of the potential conditions that might enhance or reduce intergenerational solidarity at the micro- or macro-structural level are dealt here in brief. McPherson (1983: 263) identified three processes within family that affect intergenerational solidarity. They are, (i) the expected frequency of interaction between generation; (ii) the similarities in values between generation; and (iii) frequency of helping relation between generation. Presence of these processes in a family would lead to intergenerational solidarity and absence of anyone of these processes will lead to strain and conflict between generations (Bengtson & Black, 1973; Bengtson & Cutler, 1976; Bengtson & Scharder, 1982; Troll, 1980). Intergenerational solidarity within family includes whole range of shared domestic affective and financial services between them. The limits of this kinship ties are still poorly defined between generations and are related to mutual aid within family, material aspect of harmony and the whole family working for the whole family, rather than one member of another).

Legors (2002 : 258) argued that norms of reciprocity, their acceptance and practice in accordance with the circumstances defined by individual needs resources or capacity is a significant factor in facilitating solidarity within family and between generations. It is also inclusive as all the members of the family, belonging to different generations are working in the interest of the total family but not of a part.

According to Robbert, Richards and Bengtson (1991), intergenerational solidarity can be identified on the basis of six elements. They are:

- *Associational solidarity* (frequency and pattern of interaction between family members in various family activities).
- *Affectual solidarity* (type and degree of positive sentiment held about family members and degree of reciprocity of these sentiments).
- *Consensual solidarity* (degree of agreement of values, attitudes and belief among family members).
- *Functional solidarity* (degree of helping and exchange of resources).
- *Normative solidarity* (strength of commitment to performance of familial roles and to meeting familial obligation or familism).
- *Structural solidarity* (opportunity structure of intergenerational relationship reflected in number, type and geographic proximity of family members).

Thus, the focus is on reciprocal support. Three types of support are identified. They are: practical support that generations give to each other, in terms of helping, caring, financial support and social support.

Rossi and Rossi (1990) studied parent-child relationships and found that pointed out history of family relations might have a significant effect on family solidarity at a later stage of life. They argue that in the case of lack of adequate early parental child closeness or bond, no subsequent events later in life can develop the required bond between them or compensate the early missing link between generations. The presence of solidarity reflects the positive aspect of varying living arrangement family structure (Lowenstein Katz, Deatland & Bazo, 2001).

Lowenstein (2002) studied households comprised three generations. He developed various dimensions that emerged from his analysis of data as a central theme that reflects intergenerational solidarity. Seven dimensions emerged from the analysis of data. The dimensions are: (a) division of labour regarding household chores and care of grandchildren (functional and normative solidarity); (b) management of household finances (functional solidarity only); (c) economic and housing issues (functional solidarity only); (d) emotional support and care (affectual solidarity); (e) involvement in the intimate social relationships of other generations (affectual solidarity); (f) space and privacy (normative solidarity); and finally (g) education of grandchildren and transmission of values (normative solidarity).

Cuyvers (2000) observed two types of solidarity between generations in families. First type of generational solidarity is known as *reciprocal solidarity* (parents look after their children and the children take care of their parents when they grow old). The second type of intergenerational solidarity is known as *chain solidarity* (the children in due course will become parents, the care for the aging parents will be of less concern to them).

Quortrup (2000) argued that the cost of raising children have been increasingly privatized while the benefits have been socialized in both intergenerational and intergenerational perspectives, leading to increasing polarization between people who have children and the ones who do not. Intergenerational solidarity is changing into pure chain solidarity, where people are only interested in the well-being of their offspring rather than their aging parents. Thus, generational solidarity is understood as a reciprocal phenomenon in terms of support (practical, financial assistance and social) provided by the children to their elderly parents and *vice versa*, (Taniguchi, *et al.*, 2017). Research shows that family members tend to provide support to maintain solidarity based on needs of the recipient, (Lennartsson, *et al.*, 2010).

Drury, *et al.*, (2016) argued that "perceived quality of intergenerational contact has positive effects on the well-being of the older generations and have the potential to reduce ageism and the frequency of contact is not a sufficient condition to promote the well-being of older generations."

Inter-Generational Ambivalence

Intergeneration relation studies have emphasized mostly on the presence and/or absence of solidarity or conflict within the family, but these two modes of intergenerational relations fail to capture the complexity of love and hate towards members of different generations in the family (Lüscher, 1998; Lüscher & Pillemer, 1998; Marshall *et al.*, 1993). In order to understand this complexity, a new concept, intergenerational ambivalence was derived.

Bleuler (1991) was the first person who coined the word ambivalence; later, Freud in psycho-analysis applied the term to the situation where the feeling of love and hate exist. The term was later extended to societal level (Merton & Barber, 1963 : 95) in compatible normative expectation of attitudes and beliefs and behaviour. Individual and society are embedded with status and roles. Ambivalence is more manifested in condition where the role partners have conflicting role expectations. Such ambivalent behaviours are observed among close relationships like father and son. In the context of father-son relationship, father prefers independence of his son from him and simultaneously father resists relinquishing his authority. Lüscher & Pillemer (1998) identified the ambivalent relation at social structural level in terms of institutions, resources and requirement status, roles and norms and at subjective level through cognition, emotion and motivation. Lendon (2017) found that there is a decline in ambivalence over time with different patterns by generation, cohort/life stage, and gender. Further, children experience greater levels of ambivalence than parents and there is a reciprocal influence of ambivalence between them.

Thus, uncertainty and lack of clarity may contribute to ambivalent relationship in the family; both positive and negative feelings coexist towards same individual or object. Such contrary feelings play a significant role in determining the pattern of intergenerational relations (Thompson & Holmes, 1996). Three aspects may influence ambivalent behaviour/relation between parents and their children. They are : (i) autonomy *vs*. dependency, (ii) conflicting norms, (iii) solidarity and ambivalence (Lüscher & Pillemer, 1998).

Autonomy vs. *Dependency*: Autonomy and dependency are two poles of ambivalence in the intergenerational relations. These two contrary needs presents itself into the structure of the period, status of parents and young adult. Particularly, in adulthood, ambivalence comes to play with the emergence of contradicting demands of parental need for help, support and nurturance from their children and their children's desire for freedom and distance from them exists between the desire of parents from their adult children for help, support and nurturance (Cohler, 1983; Cohler & Altergott, 1995; Moss & Moss, 1992).

In context of ambivalence, autonomy *vs.* dependency has three major trends that determine the ambivalent relation:

- Freedom and Authority of generation.
- Role allocation (child rearing practices).
- Autonomy of old generation.

Older people want autonomy and also they want to be dependent at the same time. When their autonomy is threatened, it leads to and gives rise to stress, giving rise to ambivalent situation. In role allocation when children are close to mother they are close, but the differences in upbringing process could generate conflict and give rise to ambivalence. In context of freedom and authority, when the elderly motivate their children to be independent, but do not compromise with their authority, this conflict promotes ambivalence.

Conflicting Norms Regarding Intergenerational Relations: Norms entail widely accepted rules that specify appropriate behaviours in particular circumstances. These rules state how individual in certain social position are obligated to think or act.

George (1986) showed four complex and ambivalent situations that created distress and influence.

- Biological based factors (Parent-child attachment).
- Socialization factor (The fact that majority of the caregivers are women who had been socialized into taking up nurturing and supporting roles.
- Competing roles (Daughter *vs.* wife and mother).
- Countervailing social norms (Solidarity *vs.* reciprocity).

Out of these four, two generate conflicts, i.e. reciprocity and solidarity. For example, father needs support of his children in protection in crisis, but son looks for reciprocity. If the father-son maintains reciprocity and mutual support, the situation promotes ambivalence.

The literature in gerontology reveals mutual dependency, financial assistance leading to ambivalence. When the younger generation neglects the elderly in mutual dependency, then elderly feel physically abused and when younger person feels powerless and dependent, then they feel abused by their old aged parents.

Also, they bear the weight of family obligation and normative obligation which can be seen as solidarity or ambivalence.

Intergenerational Relations and Habitat

At the end of the year 2005, cities and towns will inhabit almost half of the world's population (Hall, *et al.*, 1996). With an increase in the population of aged citizens and diverse experiences (Bell, 1997), aging is emerging as an urban policy in developing countries (Sen, 1994). According to Tripathi (1987), urbanization is changing the structure of family. Such changes in the structure of family are resulting in changes in the obligations and decision-making, the relationship between husband and wife and the socialization of children. Conflicts were observed in the area of traditional family structure, level of hierarchy, role of women, parent child relation and sexual frustration.

Gerontologists have been interested in comprehending the impact of climate differences in services and lifestyles in the rural and urban areas, availability of neighbourhood, support network, size of community, access to social recreational and health services and on individuals' behaviour and well-being.

Rural aged have not been studied to the same extant as the urban aged (Youmans, 1963, 1977; Ansello, 1980; Kim & Wilson, 1981), rather inferences have been drawn from the urban studies as to how the rural environment differs from the urban, and what impact these differences have on the aging rural residents.

The life style of a cultivator differs from that of a businessman or a mechanic in a small town or village. The life of cultivator and small businessman may be less structured with leisure time and he may not retire until his health declines (Keating and Marshal,1980). A further distinction must be drawn between improved, traditional and substance rural setting (Gordner, 1981). Fengler & Jonsen (1981) found that life satisfaction is more among rural elderly than the urban elderly. These differences are attributed to a greater frequency and quality of interaction with friends and neighbours to a lower incidence of crime and a smaller community size. Besides these factors, rural elderly receive informal support from neighbours. The rural elderly may perceive and experience relatively less economic deprivation than younger member, because they live in an environment of a lower average per capita income and lower cost of living. Some urban elderly express their dissatisfaction on the basis of perceived real or imagined economic deprivation than the younger age group that live in more affluent urban areas.

Goldstein *et al.* (1983) study in Kathmandu (Nepal) reveals that membership in an extended family provides security and satisfaction for the elderly persons. It is an oversimplification. Though older people in the Hindu culture living with their children and grandchildren respect and care for them, but the household composition indicates more complex reality. Whilst majority of the older people living in extended families with resources and assets are in a stronger position to draw reciprocal support from family, the wider structural constraints will shape the nature of intergenerational relations in family. For instance, urban younger aged sample of Kathmandu feels that their capacity to meet cultural expectations and reciprocal obligation has been reduced between generations in family, as a consequence of low wages, higher inflation and unemployment rates. The elderly persons, dependent economically on their children, felt least happy than those elderly who provide economic contribution to their family.

Heslop's (1995) study was conducted on older people in the urban area of Durban and rural setting of Mobodhongwa, North province, South Africa. The main aim of the study was to assess the needs of older peoples and the resources available locally to meet out those needs, and also to share experiences and ideas to find ways of working within communities, income security assess to health care and literacy is important to achieve an adequate level of well-being. He found pensions as a major source of income and security. However, access to their pension was limited as many hours were spent in the long queues in cold weather and during the time of ill health too.

Vera Sanso (2000) conducted a study in Tamil Nadu to realize differences in the intergenerational relations between rural and urban areas. One of the striking differences in thus was observed is the caste based residential segregation which is predominant in rural than the urban area. Residential mobility has a significant impact on intergenerational relations. Tension in intergeneration relation in poor families is a consequence of irregular and low income. Urban poor families feel pressure between family income and demands to increase their status that results in tensions and conflicts between generations. When social scientist and gerontologist have tried to understand aging and the social process, they found economy to be the key point. Many studies show class differences in frequency type of exchanger (Troll & Bengtson, 1979; Newgarten, 1979; Lacy & Hendricks, 1980).

Shans (1967) studied family help patterns among 2,500 people. He found reciprocal assistance among 645 members on different social class, but size of family living arrangements; family values and economic position vary in social class accordance. Also with the amount, frequencies of mutual aids vary. Reciprocity is more commonly founded among working class people with face to face interaction between the generations. However, social exchange patterns are observed among middle class with telephonic-based interaction between generation as a consequence of social mobility and geographical distance (McPherson, 1973 : 337).

Socialization patterns vary in accordance with the social class of the parents. The middle class inculcates values of hard work, autonomy, self-direction, while working class parents emphasize on values of conformity and obedience in the child rearing practices (Kohn, 1963, 1969).

The socialization practices and inculcation of certain values to the children related with Structural Factor like level of education and occupation of parents may influence the socialization practices. For instance, curiosity as a value is preferred value inculcated by the parents with higher education to their children. They do not favour conformity and self-discipline. Educated fathers inculcate values of curiosity. Mothers with senior high school education, adopt rearing practices that promote conformity. Mothers with lower occupation prefer self-constraints.

The quality of marital relation among intergenerational interaction is affected by economic distress and experience of the family affects intergenerational relations through the quality of marital relations (Conger *et al.*, 1993).

Intergenerational Relations and Coping

Review of literature on the relation between nature of intergeneration relation and patterns of coping indicates four possible patterns of coping behaviour in response to specific stressful events and intergenerational conflict (Steinman, 1979). First is the "Overcurious Approach". The younger generation helps their parents with excessive energy and resources at the exclusion of personal need and interest to minimize the conflicts with their parents. But this approach may create stress and interpersonal problem with the spouse and children, as they possibly feel neglected. Second, the "Active Avoiders", where interaction is avoided and alternative care systems are looked to the old aged. Thus, this may often give rise to a feeling of guilt. Third, the Vacillator, whose over zealousness and subsequent stress and followed by avoidance and subsequent guilt, which then leads to overzealous involvement and the repetition of the cycle of vacillation. Finally, the "Constructive Approach" where the younger generation seeks assistance from friends and professionals, counsellor to reduce the conflicts and to facilitate frequency and quality of interactions. These patterns only suggest the reaction of children to the intergenerational conflict. However, fewer empirical studies have been conducted to support this approach. Two broad coping strategies are noted on the basis of stressful event and coping adopted. They are: avoidance (active or passive) and problem solving or emotional focused coping (Carver & Scheir, 1994; Lazarus & Folkman, 1984).

Cross (1995) categorized the coping strategies or direct and indirect in the context of family conflict. In direct coping strategy, stressful demands are dissolved through own effort like problem-solving and support seeking. In indirect coping strategy, adjustment of self to the stressful demands is emphasized. Change in situations like forbearance and self-direction is not emphasized. European societies with individualistic values predominately favour direct coping but in collectivistic social milieus, such direct coping may be preferably avoided and indirect coping strategies are considered more appropriate (Weisz, Rothbaum & Blackburn, 1984).

Asian American and Hispanic employees have adopted more indirect coping strategies in response to stressful demands (Diaz-Guerreo, 1967; Weisz *et al.*, 1984).

Chang (1996), in his comparative study on Asian American and Caucasian college going students, found that Asian American college students used social withdrawal and problem avoidance as coping strategies more than the Caucasians and also these indirect coping strategies may not be linked to psychological maladjustment. South East Asian refugees in the context of ethnic discrimination adopted indirect coping strategies (Non, Beiser, Kaspar, Hou & Rummens, 1999), while Hispanics mostly used direct coping strategies like depending on family relations, seeking support from friends and indirect coping orientation like spiritual inclination in different circumstances (Abraido-lanze, Guier & Revenson, 1996; Yeh & Wang, 2000).

However, studies that have a narrow focus in intergenerational conflict present a limited and mixed view in different cultural groups. Aldwin & Greenbergen's (1987) study on Korean Americans, demonstrates the significant rate at which reframing as a coping strategy was adopted when children perceived their parents as conservative, whereas European Americans used the coping strategy of acceptance in similar cases.

In the study Mena Padilla and Maldonado (1987) of immigrants and later generation college student across ethnic groups it was found that early immigrants, late immigrants and second or third generation students all resort to direct coping strategies while dealing with family acculturation conflict. For instance, strategies like active, planning and seeking support from others etc.

Chang (2001) considered problem-solving as an active engagement in analyzing and solving the problem that seeks social and emotional support from others. The effectiveness of this coping strategy depends on the context, but not inherent in the strategies (Uba, 1994), that regulate, the emotions and facilitate comforts with that of others (Cutrona & Russel, 1990; Lazarus and Folkman, 1984).

O'Brien, Margalin & John (1995) argue that problem solving as a process may prove to be psychologically taxing and can lead to increasing levels of stress in association with the conflict as family conflicts often remain unresolved despite the measures taken in response to it.

Lee and Liu (2001) found evidence for the engagement of Asian American students in more approach-oriented coping such as self-direction, denial, disengagement, emotional venting, and substance use to manage family conflict. However, avoidance oriented coping was linked to greater psychological distress.

Out of all these sources of conflict, how the coping strategies vary between different class and habitat (rural/urban, socio-economic conditions) need a systematic comprehension.

Indian Perspective on Intergenerational Relations

In India, the majority of the studies in the area of intergenerational relations is represented by the works of Rath, 1971; Sinha, 1972; Gangrade, 1975; where the attention has been given to the area of generation gap with respect to differential values and attitudes among generations. Rath (1971) in his study have found striking differences in those of the values adopted by the young *versus* that of the old. He found that older generation to have a positive attitude towards religion and negative attitude towards science, however, the opposite is true for younger generation. The younger and older generations also construe god and religion very differently (Mishra & Prasad, 1978). However, there is also evidence for similarity in views where members of both the generations have discriminatory attitudes towards the old suggesting the minority group position of the elderly. Apart from the differences that separate the young and the old, there has also been other factors that can lead to intergenerational conflict. Some of them are financial insecurity, stress regarding future, perception of the existing problem, activities undertaken within a particular role position of elderly in the family and as well as their status (Prakash, 1996). Moreover, researches also suggest that the existence of shared values norms and cultural traditions that manifests in shared activities such as grandparents sharing the child care role and socalization with that of the parents or participation in other family processes leads to solidarity and satisfaction (Chaddha & Mongia,1997; Chaddha & Kolt, 2004; Panda, 2004; Sonar & Prasad, 2004). However Versa-Sanso, (2007) suggest that this pattern of intergenerational relations has some inherent drawbacks due to the usual non-fulfilment of reciprocity of obligation. Even though the members of the older generation extends support, the younger generation fails to reciprocate this support by providing the needed physical, emotional and financial support. Moreover, this situation worsens when the members of the younger generations indulges themselves in deviant expenditure through involvement in gambling, substance abuse and fail to support the family due to their lack of desire to work non-involvement in work, deviant expenditure on gambling, drinking, substance abuse does not contribute to the subsistence need of the family but nevertheless, they expect contribution from the older generation leading to exchange of word (verbal abuse), and sometimes even to physical violence.

Another facet of the study is the relationship between factors such as demographic variables like location (rural/urban) and level of education with that of intergenerational relations. It was found that intergenerational support is more prevalent in rural areas than in urban settings. On the other hand, generation gap was more pronounced among urban families (Martin, 1990; Mishra & Tiwari,1980; Bhingradiya & Kamla, 1997). With respect to education, it was found that the younger generations hold negative attitudes towards the elderly and this prejudice becomes more pronounced with increasing education levels (Vermani & Sharma, 1979). However, Bhingradiya & Kamala (1997) argue against the position advocated by that of Vermani and Sharma and contend that Education and modernization leads to reduction in intergenerational conflicts. Verma & Satanarayana (2012) also found evidence for the influence of family economic condition and location (rural/urban) on the pattern of intergenerational relations.

Intergenerational Relations and Well-being

The nature of Intergenerational relations within the family has emerged as one of the important potential sources of well-being. The cohesive intergenerational relation is probably as important as the issue of their pensions. Moreover, literature suggests that practical support which the children extend to their aged parents, promote better mental and physical well-being.

The literature on intergenerational relations and the impact of social support exchange in the old age reveals contrary psychological consequences (Krause, 1986; Russel & Cutrona, 1991). Silverstein and Bengtson (1994) found that social support improves psychological well-being or buffers the impact of stressful events, but others (Dean, Kolodny & Wood, 1990; Kruase, Ling & Keith,1990; Lee & Ellithorpe,1982) have found that social support has little bearing on well-being of older generations in Intergenerational relations. However, several findings report that that the elderly who received support from their children for the satisfaction of basic needs, felt loss of autonomy and stress among them (Arling, 1987; Dunham, 1995; Green & Feld, 1989; Lee, Netzer & Coward, 1995; Penning & Strain, 1994).

Silverstein and Bangtson (1994) have found that parents generally preferred to remain functionally autonomous as far as possible before relying on their adult children for support. In fact, the elderly generally expected less support than their children were willing to provide. Indeed, higher intensity of social support might cause painful relationships between parent and children around the difficult issues of role reversals (Chappell, 1991).

However, Bengtson & Kuyper (1986) found that vigorous social support makes elderly persons vulnerable, resulting not only in greater dependency, but also degradation of their skills and competence. Such degradation of skills and competence further increases vulnerability and emotional distress. Coyne, Wortman & Lehman (1988) observed that moderate emotional support from adult children to their aged parents buffers the well-being of older people. However, higher emotional support failed to do so (Krause, 1995). Sometimes, the old-age people extend support to their adult children, in such cases, older parents experienced higher intensity of well-being than the parents who were not providing support to their adult children. It also helps to develop productive social roles and, intimacy between parents and their children (Beckman, 1981; Kessler, McLeod & Wethhington, 1985; Krause, Herzogn & Baker, 1992; Shumaer & Brownell, 1984).

Once the children enter college, they develop greater autonomy and independence while parents lose control and authority over their children during this period. This is also the period when parents and children reconcile such differences that result in the decline of family conflicts and consequently, promote psychological well-being (Greenberg & Chen, 1996; Laursen & Collins, 1994).

In India, in the context of collectivistic values and affiliation oriented society, the relations between grandparents and grandchildren are friendly, involving discussions around issues of common interest, carrier, plans and future goals etc. (Suri & Chaddha, 2003). Singh and Chaddha (2004) conducted a study to understand the intergenerational relationship from the perspective of life satisfaction, attitude and role expectation of the grandchildren towards their grandparents and *vice versa*, no difference was found in terms of role expectation and hope for health, interaction between generations. Whereas Rikhye & Chadda (1998) found no such impact of generation gap on the well-being of elderly in Indian families. The distance between the young and old was mainly due to differences in their interests, likes and dislikes, ideas and practices, and their self-concepts and self-regard. Opposing and protesting attitude among the youth are common as they prefer to live as per their own will, rather than listening to and obeying the old. These attitudes have been reported as generated distance between the generations (Rammurti, 2002; Raju, 2002). Most of the younger generations felt that the expenditure made on health of their aged parents was a wasteful investment; in many cases it was found that younger members failed to take care of their aged parents. The failure to take care of elderly led to certain differences between the young and the old (Rammurti, 2002). Therefore, the psychological, physical and health aspects of the aged have a bearing on the intergenerational relations.

In 2007, a special issue on "Intergenerational Relations: Theory Research and Policy," published by *Journal of Social Issue*, emphasized the relationship between intergenerational relations, processes and well-being. In this issue, it was argued that increased life expectancy would lead to increase in the frequency of generations staying within the family, which can have direct impact of the pattern of intergenerational relationships within the existing social setting. Ajrouch (2007) addressed the significance of intergenerational contact for the well-being of the members of older generations, as well as the implication of dynamic structure on the increasing educational resources of younger generations. Besides, the changing structure of intergenerational relationships affect the families in significant ways: divorce, remarriage, cohabitation, the expansion of in-laws familial ties, and trans nationality which affect the family and individual well-being (Santos & Levitt, 2007), whereas grandparents play a vital role in child rearing (Ruiz & Silverstein, 2007). Besides this, Lowenstein, Katz & Gur-Yaish (2007) find that maintaining mutual support and exchanges is very important motivation for the predictors of well-being of all family members and generations.

Conclusion and Further Research

The existing literature shows that the intergenerational generational research came into light with the emergence of area of gerontology and social aging. The review also suggests that the patterns of study were influenced by time's perspective and discipline's perspective (Sociology, Psychology & Anthropology). The study started with generation gap, followed by generational conflict, solidarity and ambivalence from 1956 to present times. Apart from this, the studies covered feeling, experience and well-being of people during intergenerational interaction, coping strategies used by people to maintain intergenerational relations during interaction, and role of location (rural and urban) to influence the intergenerational relations.

Moving to present scenario, the intergenerational relations studies see a worldwide increase in interest and the academic institutions have taken more initiatives in this regard. Some other important markers are: Two special issues on intergenerational relations by *Journal of Social Issues*. In 1974, the journal had published 2 special issues and focused on the effects of social change on intergenerational relations, and more recently in 2007, the journal once again published special issue and emphasized on the intergenerational relations and well-being. In 2004, *Indian Journal of Gerontology* had published special issues and focused on pattern and process of intergenerational relations in Indian context. In 2012, *Journal of Advance Life Course Research* published special issue on intergenerational relations which covers intergenerational relations across life course, with much emphasis on recent trends of study (Steinbach, 2012); generations connection across the life course which emphasizes how strong is the solidarity between family generations (Szydlik, 2012). However, Min, Silverstein & Lendon (2012) emphasized on intergenerational transmission of values over the family life course and emphasized on role of socialization in life course; beside this, another issues are taken into consideration, i.e. continuity and change in Intergenerational family relationship (Schenk & Dkstra, 2012); importance of grandparents' role from class specific respondent (Mahne & Kingebiel, 2012). Besides, the special issues Tailor and Francis published *Journal of Intergenerational Relations* which emphasizes only on intergenerational issues. However, another *Journal of Marriage and Family*, published by Willey & Sons, covers various issues of intergenerational relations. After going through literature and apart from above mentioned issues, following trends need to be studied:

- Need to study Intergenerational relations in inter-discipline perspective.
- Use indigenized method to study the phenomena in cultural context.
- Need to study younger generation problem in Intergenerational research.
- Role of demographic variable to determine the Intergenerational relations.
- Explore the factors which affect Intergenerational relations in cultural context.
- Use of coping strategies by generations to maintain Intergenerational relations (Pillmer, 2010).
- Cognitive and Emotional aspects of Intergenerational relations.
- Role of parenting and schooling in Intergenerational support.
- Effect of Aging policies on Intergenerational relations.

2
Method and Methodologies in Intergenerational Relations

This chapter deals with the methodological issues in Intergenerational Relations research and delineates the various methods and the sample of this particular study. Chapter 1 deals with the empirical journey of Intergenerational Relational studies and emphasized that the issues of study varied with changing time and place. Review of literature reveals that generation gap or difference, generational conflict, solidarity or ambivalence exist in Intergenerational relations. During the era between 1950 and 1975, gerontologists and social scientists tried to understand the generation gap on the bases of value differences, political opinion, opinion about nuclear war, changing life style and opinion about love and arrange marriage (Pitts, 1969; Orum, 1972; Altbach & Peterson, 1972; Yankelovich, 1972; Rokeach,1973; Bengtson, *et al.*, 1974). The authors selected sample from cohorts or students using survey method.

In the era between 1975 and 1990, most of the studies in the intergenerational area generally had in the title the phrase "Across generation", primarily focusing on perception and attitudes towards each other between generations—how the younger generation perceive the older generation or aging? (Butler, 1969; McTavish, 1971; Anantharaman, 1979; Green, 1981; Kite & Johnsons, 1988).

After 1990s, the focus shifted to the study of nature of Intergenerational Relations and much emphasis was given to generational conflict (Uba,1994; Laursen & Collins,1994; Laursen, Coy & Collins,1998; Arnett,1999; Fuligini, Tseng & Lam, 1999).

They attributed that generational conflict is a consequence of generation gap, in terms of differences in values and attitudes between the generations. In case of immigrants, intergenerational conflict has been attributed to culture specific patterns of parenting techniques, like western values and lifestyles, the feelings of obstruction of autonomy and independence among younger generation by older generations. Some researchers have pointed out that generally it is not only conflict, but also generational solidarity that characterized intergeneration relations (Bengtson and Black,1973; Bengtson and Cutler, 1976; Bengtson & Schroder,1978; Rossi & Rossi, 1990; Legors, 2002; Bengtson *et al.*, 2002; Komter & Vellebergh, 2002; Lowestin, 2002; Merz, 2005), depending on the similarities of attitudes and values between generations. These scholars selected family as a unit in their studies and have mostly emphasized on the three generations within a family (grandfather, father and son), using survey method in general. In the mid-1990s, the focus of intergenerational studies was on ambivalence (Luscher, 1998; Luscher & Pillmer, 1998; Thompson and Hoslem, 1996). They argued and emphasized that ambivalence is mostly manifested in close relationships in which partners have conflicting role expectations. Thus, the focus shifted from conflict to solidarity to ambivalence. Besides this, social scientists have also studied the psycho-social consequences of intergenerational relations. Such researches on intergenerational relations used diverse research designs, that have been discussed below.

Cross Sectional Design: Being least costly in terms of time and money this design has been widely used by social scientists. As per the design data was collected from individuals and analysis and reporting of data was done group-wise.

Longitudinal Research Design: In this design, research was conducted on an individual or group for several years to study the aging process and to identify the age related changes in individual or group. Longitudinal design can give more accurate and complete result. Because individuals or groups are observed over a given time period, it yields direct evidence with respect to changes in individual or group (Bengtson, 1971, 2002; Palmore, 1981; Mednick,Harway & Finello, 1984; Brannens, *et al.*, 2004; Brannens, J., 2006).

Cohort Analysis: This design covers the maturational changes, cohort differences and environmental (time and cultural) effect, thereby reducing the confusion of age changes with age differences. In this process, similar information is obtained about individuals who were born in different times and also measured at different times (Schaie, 1965; Glean, 1977; Hasting and Berry, 1979).

Life History Method: This was used to study the experiences of different generations in the same family (Brannen *et al.*, 2002).

Sampling

In any research representative sample is required for the validity of research. When population has special characteristic or research problem needs specific sample, it is difficult to derive representative probability sample through random selection. In the intergenerational relations research different samples and measures were selected as per objective. For example, in early years during 1950 to 1970 major emphasis was on generation gap and generational conflict. To study these issues, cross sectional as well as cohort analysis method was used and the sample comprised older generation and younger generation as two generational groups. A number of studies were done on teachers and students as they represented the two different generations for studying the attitude towards political opinion, religion, science, values, changing life style (Gangrade, 1975 ; Sinha, 1972; Rath,1971; Tiwari & Mishra,1979; Mishra & Tiwari, 1980). Besides this, after 1970's there was a change in objectives with major emphasis on intergenerational conflict, intergenerational perception of each other and intergenerational solidarity, and status of elderly within the family and society. Research design was cross-sectional and cohort design analysis, and sample comprised older as well as younger generation. After 1990s emphasis was on solidarity type of relationship, ambivalence type of relationship, psycho-social consequences of intergenerational relations, how generations perceive their status, authority and autonomy in the family. The method which was used in these studies was survey method and qualitative method (life history, interview etc.). Sample included older generation and younger generation, and in some cases generations from the same family.

In India, family is the most important institution that has survived through the ages. India has a documented heritage of stable family life and structure which has been able to withstand the vicissitudes over the centuries (Sinha, 1984). Indian family, like most families in Oriental cultures, is considered to be strong, well knit, and resilient and enduring. It is, however, important to point out that although families might be strong and resilient; heterogeneity and diversity characterize the family life in India.

The demographic transitions suggest that many families would now have multiple generations living together at a certain point of time. Family members will spend more time in intergenerational roles requiring negotiations and understanding in dealing with change. Thus, intergenerational relation is a zeitgeist process that change social strata. Most of the studies on intergenerational relations have focused on society; few studies have focused on family. Mostly, studies select father, son, daughter, mother and grandson and granddaughter as sample and try to understand the relationship through changing time perspective. However, keeping recent times in mind, a number of other factors (need, changing priority, economic factor, authority and its loss, autonomy and dependency etc.) influence the nature of intergeneration relationship apart from the changing time perspective. Another issue that has attracted attention of social scientists is the study of the process of intergenerational relations; on what issues generations interact with one another, how they handle problems emanating from inter-generational interactions or what coping strategies they adopt during stressful situations of such kinds. Use of indigenized method to study intergenerational phenomena in the local cultural context has also been stressed. Keeping these arguments in mind this study used mixed method research that employs both qualitative and quantitative method. Under the qualitative genre narrative as a method was used to study pattern and process of intergenerational relations. In quantitative method, survey method and questionnaire was used to see the effect of intergenerational relations on well-being.

The Approach

A clear distinction has been drawn between variable-based (quantitative) and person based (qualitative) methods in researches on stress (Spicer, 1997; Magnusson & Toresterd, 1993). Variable based researches formulate research questions around a set of concepts that reflect only few aspects of individual functioning. They also tend to reduce the dynamics of stress process to patterns of empirical relationships between variables (Somerfield, 1997a) that can be tested through the relationship between variables in multivariate statistical analysis. They have a limited role in exploring the dynamics of the stress process than was previously assumed. Person based methods, on the other hand, give pivotal importance to the various experiences, meanings and interpretations of individual placed in a particular social position and context rather than variables as the central focus of data collection and analysis. Qualitative methodologies yield rich descriptive data about individuals, their functioning and contextual richness of the stress process (Somerfield, 1997; Spicer, 1997; Thoists, 1995). Sole reliance on either quantitative or qualitative method may restrict the ability for in-depth exploration of certain dimensions of stress experience (Morgan & Smircich, 1980). So, a combination of qualitative and quantitative method may provide insights into the transactional stress-coping processes (Cooper, Dewe & O'Driscoll, 2001).

It is also important to recognize that as the complexity of phenomena increases, the measurement of certain aspect of models may require the use of qualitative methods (Das, 1983), or at the very least a combination of methods. Stress is not a monolithic experience (Cox & Howarth, 1990), so, it is difficult to convert it into quantity. Stress has a context, not only individual, institutional or cultural, but also involves interpretations of individual's physical experiences of the stress. Qualitative method can capture the meanings and also the contextual issues related to the stress process. Thus, useful data can be generated through a balanced combination of qualitative and quantitative methods (Pfeffer, 1990).

Advantages of Combining Methods

Rank (1992) identified the following advantages of combining these two methods:

1. Complementary: The term complementary is defined by Webster (1974) as "mutually supporting each other's" 'lacking'. The integration of qualitative and quantitative data fits such a description in that their strength and weaknesses are largely opposite to each other. Methodologically speaking, a strong argument can be made for such integration. The strength of qualitative method lies in generating data that has richness and depth through verbatim transcripts from in-depth interviews and field notes and documents. It also allows the participants to structure the world as they see significance appeal, rather than as the researcher views. In this way the researchers can acquire a deeper understanding of a particular phenomenon. The two paradigms (qualitative and quantitative) tend to complement each other and lead to new and different knowledge. In the present study on intergenerational relations data were collected through narratives generated from in-depth interviews and observations (qualitative) and the effect of intergenerational relations on well-being has been studied with the help of questionnaire (quantitative method).

2. *Additional Insight:* Blending of quantitative and qualitative methods in research provides additional insights in terms of theoretical perspectives, methodological approaches and the ways in which respondents are viewing and interpreting the world. Through such combination of methods we can grasp different aspects of reality.

According to Bryman (1988) qualitative research can reveal regularities in social life while quantitative evidence can find the relations between variables. Quantitative data were effectively used in relating specific consequences of caring mentally ill family member on care givers. The qualitative data acquired from in-depth interviews, on the other hand, revealed regularities of those consequences. These two methods jointly provide richer understanding and insight into research topic.

3. *Increased Validity*: It also enhances the potential validity of the findings. Consistent results with the qualitative and quantitative methods lead to greater validity of findings and researcher's confidence in the results.

4. *Pushing the Research Further:* The combined use of qualitative and quantitative methods in research sometimes leads to discrepancies. Such incongruent findings, work as a springboard for further investigations into the causes behind the discrepancy in the findings (Bryman, 1988a). Such probing further reformulates both the hypothesis and the research design.

Integration of qualitative and quantitative methods will strengthen the research design and analysis, it also provides greater insights, enhances validity and the potential for redirecting the inquiry. The blending of these two methods provides a powerful tool for understanding the process and dynamics behind family life.

Both qualitative and quantitative methods were used to capture the diverse experiences of families located in heterogeneous socio-economic settings as propounded by Rank (1992).

An overview of journals and books dealing with family studies reveals that they have used either qualitative or quantitative method. Combination of both qualitative and quantitative research design and analysis has the potential for improvements in the construction, execution and analysis of family issues. Qualitative methods are used to understand the heterogeneous meanings interpretations and subjective experiences of family members (Weber, 1974). The contributions of qualitative methodologies in the comprehension of the dynamics and intergenerational relations in family have been well documented (La Rossa & Wolfe, 1985). The focus of qualitative methods is to identify the processes that create and sustain the family reality. It also deals with individual and phenomenological experiences of family members. Families are groups that construct shared meanings. This method is particularly useful in understanding the experiences of caregivers, and stressors that they undergo while dealing with a mentally ill family member, and impact on family functioning and intergenerational relations. Through qualitative methods, we can observe patterns of interactions and the ongoing negotiations relating to roles, status, sharing of duties and responsibility of two or more generations among family members.

The Present Study

In the present study, keeping in mind the ongoing argument in intergenerational relations research, a combination of qualitative and quantitative methods was used for a richer understanding of the psycho-social process of intergenerational relations. To study the pattern and process of intergeneration relations as well as to understand behaviour in a cultural context the researcher has used qualitative method. Narrative method was used to collect information pertaining to family meanings and interpretations of intergenerational relationships and feeling relating to intergenerational relations. To study the effect of intergenerational relations on well-being quantitative method was used. Besides scales, socio-economic and demographic data were collected through interview schedule. These scales, interview schedules and narratives are discussed in detail in the ensuing pages.

Preliminary Pilot

In the present study a pilot fieldwork was conducted on five joint families of Allahabad city to comprehend the factors influencing the nature of intergenerational relations and their psychological consequences. From this sample, data relating to the relations between father and son, mother-in-laws and daughter-in-laws, events of joy and crisis in the family and their psychological consequences in intergenerational relations in the family, were collected through narratives. Besides this, observation sheet was also prepared to identify the socio-economic status of the family on the basis of consumption pattern and style of living.

The narratives were analysed through thematic analysis. Intergenerational relations and well-being were conceptualized on the basis of the thematic analysis and literature review. It has been realized that intergenerational relations and meaning of well-being differ across socio-economic status, and family in society. Thematic analysis of the narratives on intergenerational relations resulted in these dimension: social relations, social support, autonomy, happiness, and purpose of life. A 30-item scale was developed based on the five dimensions that emerged from thematic analysis. The dimensions and the number of items are: Social Support (6 items), Autonomy (8 items), Happiness (5 items) and for Social Relations (5 items), Purpose of Life (6 items). The scales were developed on the basis of interview data and review of literature. Some scales were adopted (for what?): Self-Esteem (7 items), Satisfaction with Life (15 items), Psychological Health (11 items), and Physical health (10 items). For the socio-economic status the data collected through observation sheet on life style and consumption pattern of the randomly selected families were analysed.

Judges Ratings

Thirteen judges, five faculty members and ten research scholars from Centre for Advanced Studies in Psychology (Allahabad University) were contacted to find out the face validity of the items in a dimension. The judges were requested to provide their comments on the appropriateness of item pertaining to each dimension on the basis of the following:

- Ambiguity, social desirability, redundancy and repetition of each item; the language, clarity of instructions, and to scale points against each item.
- Items on the dimension of well-being were jumbled up and the judges were requested to indicate the category/dimension to which a particular item belongs.
- Finally, suggestions were sought on the flow of question in the Questionnaire of Well-being.

On the basis of the feedback and suggestions from the judges, necessary addition, deletion and reframing of items were made. Six items were included in social relations dimension, five items in social support, eight items in autonomy, five items in happiness and six items in purpose of life dimension.

The Pilot Testing

The questionnaire, thus evolved, was administered on 5 joint families in Allahabad city of Uttar Pradesh (India) and 5 joint families in rural areas of Soraon Tehsil of Allahabad district (India) for clarity of instructions and items. The Pilot testing also aimed to foresee the possible difriculties in data collection and to develop necessary precautions.

The Final Measures

Narrative method was used to explore the nature of intergenerational relations. Narratives were taken from respondents, related to the following points:

- Description about family members, about their behaviour and occupation.
- Differences and similarities the respondent perceived with his next generation, giving examples in terms of behaviours.

- Behavioural outcome of this relationship (tension or conflict or harmony) and how the respondent coped with these situations, with experienced examples.
- Decision-making in the family, conflicts during the process of decision-making, and how the respondents resolve this conflict (with experienced examples).

Some issues were probed which were especially related to women like:

- What are the differences and similarities in behavioural pattern related between the place of origin and the husband's house?
- Who looks after the children and prepares them for school?

The final survey questionnaire titled **Social Psychological Study on Intergenerational Relations** collected information on socio-demographic variables (gender, age, marital status, caste, religion, occupation, education of individual and family members and relation of individual to family members, nature of family, number of earning members in the family and household income). The questionnaire also collected information on other dimensions, like Self-Esteem, Social Relations, Social Support, Autonomy, Satisfaction with Life, Purpose of Life, Happiness, Health Status and Socio-Economic Status.

Socio-economic and Demographic Data

Socio-economic and demographic data relating to the nuclear, joint and extended joint type of families were collected from father/son, mother-in-law/daughter-in-law. Age, gender (male/female), level of education, marital status (married/unmarried/divorced/separated/widows), place of residence (rural/urban), religion affiliation, occupation pattern and consumption pattern, style of living and nature of relation between respondents are variables for which the data was collected through interview schedule. In the consumption pattern, data was collected in terms of ownership of air conditioner, car, television, music system, motor bike, scooter, refrigerator, washing machine etc., and their company/brand, as well as whether new items or second-hand items were purchased.

Self-Esteem Scale—Seven items were adapted from the self-esteem scale of Rosenberg (1965). These items were designed to rate the respondents' perception about oneself. A four-point rating scale ranging from 1 to 4 was used. The range of total scores varied from 7 to 28. Three items were negatively worded and responses on these items were reverse scored. A high score indicates person's high level of self-esteem and low score indicates low level of self-esteem. The alpha of the scale was found to be .82.

Social Relations—Six items were constructed for measuring social relationship with others on a four-point scale. Respondents were required to provide perception of their social relation with primary and secondary group. Total score of the scale ranged from 6 to 24. Four items were negatively worded and responses on these items were reverse scored. High score on the scale indicates that the individual is experiencing high coherent relationship with primary and secondary groups. The alpha of the scale was found to be .73.

Social Support—Five items were constructed to assess the type of support individual experiences with family members and friends on four-point scale, ranging from 1 to 4. The range of total score varied from 5 to 20. High scores indicate high level of social support a person is experiencing. The alpha of the scale was found to be .93.

Autonomy—Autonomy scale was developed to measure individual's perception about their autonomy in their family lives. Eight items measured the perception on four-point scale. The total score of the scale ranged from 8 to 32. One item was negatively worded and responses on these items were reverse scored. The alpha value of the scale is found 0.79.

Purpose of Life—Six items were developed to measure individual's perception about his life and its objective. The range of the scale varied from 6 to 24. Three items were negatively worded and responses on these items were reverse scored. The alpha value of the scale is 0.73.

Happiness—Five items were developed to measure individuals' perception about their emotional states (happiness) on a four point scale. The total score of the scale ranged from 5 to 20. One item was negatively worded and responses on these items were reverse scored. The alpha of the scale is 0.83.

Satisfaction with Life—Fifteen items were adopted from Diener's Indian version Life Satisfaction Scale representing 5 items from past, 5 from present and 5 from future. Respondents were required to provide their perception about level of satisfaction with life in the past, present and future of his/her life. To maintain the consistency of scale with other scales were measured on four-point scale in place of seven-point scale used by Diener. Total score of the scales range from 15 to 60. Alpha of the scale is 0.85.

Health—Ten items of physical health and eleven items of psychological health were selected to measure the health status of the respondent. The total score on physical health range from 10 to 40 with an alpha value of 0.92. Higher score on physical and psychological health indicates that the individual perceive high level of health problems.

Overall, Well-being scale consists of seventy three items. The range of the scale varied from 73 to 292. The alpha value of the scale is 0.88.

Table 2.1: Showing the Reliability of Well-being Scale

Variables	*No. of Items*	*Range of Score*	*Cronbach alpha*
Well-being	73	73-292	0.88
Self-esteem	7	7-28	0.82
Social relation	6	6-24	0.73
Social support	5	5-20	0.93
Autonomy	8	8-32	0.67
Purpose of life	6	6-24	0.73
Happiness	5	5-20	0.83
Satisfaction with life	15	15-60	0.85
Health Psychological	11	11-44	0.94
Physical	10	10-40	0.92

Source: Developed by the author using the data from respondents.

The study makes an endeavour to understand the process and patterns of intergenerational relations in rural and urban locations and their effect on the well-being in a comparative framework. Families living in different localities of rural and urban, with different socio-economic status were contacted. Mostly older people in the families were retired. However, some old members are still engaged in work. Members in the family belonging to younger generation work with their profiles varying from government/private service to owner of distributive agencies, shop-keeping, business, petty business, labour etc. Most women are engaged in domestic household work whereas some are teachers, and others work as domestic servants. The study intended to identify priority of values, types of crises that evolve in intergenerational relations and their coping mechanisms along with their influence on the well-being of respondents.

Socio-Economic—Socio-Economic Status refers to the relative position of a family or individual in a hierarchical social structure based on their access to/or control over, wealth, prestige, and power. Earlier measures described the occupational prestige, education level, economic position of individual.

Socio-economic status is generally considered as an important variable, both in the planning of developmental programmes and in research field in Education, Sociology, Psychology, Community Development, Agricultural Extension. Kuppuswamy (1962) prepared a scale in the context of Indian urban family and used three variables in socio-economic status scale, viz. education, occupation and income. However, Verma (1962) developed a scale for urban families and used some other variables, viz. composition of family, members' education level (particularly female members), source of income, relatives and their social position. Lewis and Dhillon (1955) evolved a scale for classifying the village families based on their socio-economic status. In his scale, he used seven factors like land owned (irrigated and not irrigated), land mortgaged, amount of credit and debt, type of house structure, income from non-agricultural occupation, ownership of livestock and bullock-cart.

Freeman (1961) measured socio-economic status of rural families in U.P. Information collected was on the basis of material possession on which items were revised to include certain other items (like watch, torch) and to exclude items which had rare occurrence so as to distinguish between high and low economic groups. The final scale consisted of the following items: land, house, and type of dwelling house, animals, iron plough and watch.

Rokeach (1973) has used income and education as an important variable in socio-economic status.

In recent studies, researchers have frequently used education level, nature of job, income, family member and caste as variables of socio-economic status. But on the basis of my personal observation, I found that in present time we cannot discriminate between families of different socio-economic status because good and moderate level of education is found in nearly every type of family and also because people do not tell their real income.

So, in the present study the socio-economic status was measured on the basis of habitat. The categories were differentiated on the basis of what materialistic goods they use, their consumption pattern and the market value of the goods purchased.

The consumption pattern shows class variation in families from different type socio-economic background. The cutting edge in urban area is AC, car, threasure which differentiated between the upper and middle class, whereas the lower class families have small TV, radio, gas, bicycle. In rural area upper class differs from middle class on the basis of car, TV, computer, generator/invertors, whereas lower class have TV, radio, bicycle, and animal.

Sample and Location

Forty eight families were selected from rural and urban areas belonging to the three socio-economic categories. From each socio-economic category 8 families were selected on the basis of purposive sampling in urban areas (Gorakhpur city) due to its large population, and randomly from rural area (Reotipur, Uttar Pradesh, India) owing to its smaller population. From each family four members—father-son, mother-in-laws, daughter-in-laws—were selected for the study. In total 185 respondents were contacted for data collection.

Gorakhpur City—Gorakhpur was a part of famous kingdom Koshal, one of the sixteen *mahajanpads* in 6th century B.C. Gorakhpur city is an ancient city of Uttar Pradesh, Gorakhpur is renowned for its ascetic Gorakhnath, who was the profounder of *Naath* sect. The city is located 265 k.m. east of the State capital Lucknow, on national highway 28. It lies between latitude 46°26′ N and longitude 83°22′ E and on the basin of rivers Rapati and Rohani. The Geographical shape of the Gorakhpur city is of a bowl shape. Total city population is 6,22,701. Out of the total population 12.00 per cent are Scheduled Caste and 0.44 per cent are Schedule Tribe population. Gender-ratio is 888 women on per 1000 men, and literacy rate of the city is 78.2 per cent. Household size is 6.7 members. 22.90 per cent are total workers in whole population and work participation is 4.4 per cent, main workers 20.5 per cent and 2.4 per cent are marginal workers. 77.1 per cent are non-workers, 0.8 per cent cultivators, 2.2 per cent Agricultural labourers, 4.5 per cent are involved in house hold industry and 92.5 per cent are involved in other works.

Table 2.2: Showing Demographic Profile of Location (Gorakhpur)

Total Population	**6,22,701**
Proportion of S.C.	12.00%
Proportion of S.T	.044%
Sex-ratio	888
Literacy rate	78.2
Household size	6.7
Total workers	22.90% (1,42,619)
Work participation	4.4%
Percentage Main workers	20.5%
Percentage of Marginal workers	2.4%
Percentage of Non-worker	77.1%
Percentage of CL	0.8%
Percentage of AL	2.2%
Percentage of HHI	4.5%
Percentage of OW	92.5%

Source: Data Bank, 2000, Economic & Statistics Section, State Planning Institute, U.P.

Reotipur—Reotipur is located on the basin of Ganga. It is situated between Ghazipur city in Uttar Pradesh and Baksar/Buxar city in Bihar state. The village has 23,307 people, out of them 19.69 per cent belonged to Scheduled Caste. Gender-ratio of the village is 930 women per 1000 men. Literacy rate is 62.7 per cent. Average size of the household in the village is 7.3 members, work participation is 27.5 per cent and 22.0 per cent are involved in main work, 5.5 per cent are involved in marginal work, 25.4 per cent are cultivators, 39.4 per cent agricultures labourers, 4.5 per cent are involved in house hold industry, 92.5 per cent involved in other works and 72.5 per cent are non-worker (Table 2.3).

Respondent—The respondents were selected from three different socio-economic status in rural and urban areas. Eight families were taken in each of the three classes in both urban and rural settings. In urban areas, there were 31 respondents from high class, in middle class there were 32 respondents and in low class there were 32 respondents. In rural areas, 28 individuals were from high class, 30 from middle class and 32 from lower class (Table 2.4).

Type of Families in Rural and Urban Areas—In urban higher socio-economic status families—23 respondents in joint families and 8 respondents lived in extended joint families. In middle socio-economic status all (32) respondents were living in joint family. In the case of urban lower socio-economic status families four belonged to nuclear, while rest lived in joint families. In case of rural participants from high socio-economic background 10 were living in joint family, while 18 lived in extended joint families. Out of 30 middle socio-economic status respondents contacted for the study, four respondents were residing in nuclear and the remaining in joint families. The entire lower socio-economic status rural respondents were residing in joint family (Table 2.5).

Table 2.3: Showing Demographic Profile of Location (Reotipur)

Total Population	**23,307**
Proportion of S.C.	19.69%
Sex-ratio	930
Literacy rate	62.7
Household size	7.3
Total workers	27.54%(6,419)
Work participation	27.5%
Percentage of Main workers	22.00%
Percentage of Marginal workers	5.5%
Percentage of Non-workers	72.5%
Percentage of CL	25.4%
Percentage of AL	39.5%
Percentage of HHI	11.00%
Percentage of OW	24.2%

Source: Data Bank, 2000, Economic & Statistics Section, State Planning Institute, U.P.

Table 2.4: Family Distribution

Location Class	*Urban*		*Rural*	
	No. of Family	*No. of People*	*No. of Family*	*No. of People*
Upper	8	31	8	28
Middle	8	32	8	30
Lower	8	32	8	32

Source: Developed by the author using the data from respondents.

Table 2.5: Type of Family in Percentage

Location & Type Class	*Urban*			*Rural*		
	Nuclear	*Joint*	*Extended Joint*	*Nuclear*	*Joint*	*Extended Joint*
Upper	0	23	8	0	10	18
Middle	0	32	0	4	26	0
Low	2	30	0	0	32	0

Source: Developed by the author using the data from respondents.

Mean Age of the Respondents: Mean age of younger male and female respondents is 31.04 and 27.54 respectively and 62.86 and 52.95 for older male and female respondents respectively in rural areas. In case of urban respondents 32.70 and 28.20 is the mean age of younger males and females while 63.95 and 55.39 for older males and females respectively (Table 2.6).

Table 2.6: Age Distribution of Respondents

Location	Younger Male			Younger Female			Older Male			Older Female		
	Mean	Sd	Range	Mean	Sd	Range	Mean	Sd	Range	Mean	Sd	Range
Rural	31.04	6.16	20-40	27.54	4.61	19-42	62.86	7.28	45-72	52.95	7.60	40-65
Urban	32.70	4.93	21-42	28.20	4.57	20-38	63.95	5.69	56-79	55.39	4.62	45-62

Source: Developed by the author using the data from respondents.

Caste Distributions of the Respondents—Analysis of respondent data on the caste basis reveals that 47.8 per cent are general, 12.2 per cent belong to other backward castes and 40 per cent belong to Scheduled Castes in rural areas. In case of urban areas 49.5 per cent of respondents belong to general categories, 16.8 per cent belong to other backward castes and 33.3 per cent belong to Scheduled Castes (Table 2.7).

Table 2.7: Caste Distribution in Percentage

Caste	Rural	Urban	Younger Male	Younger Female	Older Male	Older Female
General	47.8	49.5	45.7	47.8	53.2	47.8
OBC	12.2	16.8	17.4	15.2	10.6	15.2
SC	40.0	33.7	37.8	37.0	36.2	37.0

Source: Developed by the author using the data from respondents.

Education Profile—18.9 per cent rural respondents were illiterate, primary (6.3%), middle (4.2%), high school (18.9%). intermediate (3%), graduate (31.6%), post-graduates (10.5%), Higher studies (3.2%). In urban population the statistics was: illiterate (24.4%), primary (1.1%), middle level (4.4%), high school (11.1%), intermediate (14.4%), graduate (20%), post-graduate (14.4%), Higher studies (10%). In older male population, illiterate (12.8%), primary (8.5%), middle level (4.3%), till high school (19.1%), intermediate (21.3%), graduate (27.4%), post-graduate

(4.3%), higher studies (2.1%). In older female population, illiterate (43.5%), primary (6.5%), middle level (10.9 %), high school (15.2%), intermediate (10.9%), graduate (8.7%), post-graduate (2.2%). In younger male population, illiterate (2.2%), middle level (10.9%), high school (23.9 %.), intermediate (2.2%), graduate (41.3%), post-graduate (19.6%). In younger female, illiterate (30.4%), primary (4.3%), middle level (4.3%), high school (8.7%), intermediate (17.4%), graduate (15.2%), post-graduate (15.2 %), higher studies (4.3 %) (Table 2.8).

Table 2.8: Education Profile of Respondents in Percentage.

Education	*Rural*	*Urban*	*Older Male*	*Older Female*	*Younger Male*	*Younger Female*
Illiterate	18.9	24.4	12.8	43.5	2.2	30.4
Primary	6.3	1.1	8.5	6.5	0	4.3
Middle	4.2	4.4	4.3	10.9	10.9	4.3
High School	18.9	11.1	19.1	15.2	23.9	8.7
Intermediate	6.3	14.4	21.3	10.9	2.2	17.4
Graduate	31.6	20.0	27.4	8.7	41.3	15.2
Post Graduate	10.5	14.4	4.3	2.2	19.6	15.2
Higher Studies	3.2	10.0	2.1	0	0	4.3

Source: Developed by the author using the data from respondents.

The Job Profile—In rural areas 2.2 per cent retired as class 1, 4.4 per cent retired from class 2, 1.1 per cent working as class 2 employee, 1.1 per cent working class 4 employee, 7.8 per cent as small business 1.1 per cent in private job, 1.1 per cent in lower level private job 14.4 per cent as labour, 11.1 as cultivator, 42.2 per cent as house wife, 1.1 per cent in house hold service, 1.1 per cent in petty business, 5.6 per cent unemployed. In urban areas 3.2 per cent retired from class 1, 3.2 per cent are retired from class 2, 4.2 per cent retire from class 3, 1.1 per cent retired from big business 8.4 per cent working class 2, 2.1 per cent working class 4, 9.5 per cent big business, 4.2 per cent small business, 3.2 per cent private job, 5.3 per cent lower level private job, 1.1 per cent labour, 8.7 per cent cultivator, 42.1 per cent housewife, 3.2 per cent household service, 5.2 per cent petty business, 3.2 per cent unemployed. In case of younger males 10.9 per cent working as class 2 employee, 2.2 per cent working as class 4 employee, 15.2 per cent in big business, 13.0 per cent in small business, 6.5 per cent in private job 8.7 per cent in lower level private job 10.9 per cent as labour, 8.7 per cent in petty business, 10.9

unemployed. In case of younger females 6.5 per cent working as class 2 employee, 2.2 per cent as labour, 84.4 per cent as house wife, 6.5 per cent in house hold service. In case of older males 6.4 per cent retired from class 1, 10.6 per cent retired from class 2, 14.9 per cent retired from class 3, 2.1 per cent retired from big business, 2.1 per cent working as class 2 employee, 43 per cent are working as class 4 employee, 10.6 per cent in small business, 2.1 per cent in private job, 4.3 per cent in lower level private job. 10.6 per cent as labour, 12.8 per cent are cultivator, 2.43 per cent in petty business, 6.4 per cent unemployed. In case of older female 2.2 per cent retired from class 3, 6.5 per cent as labour, and 84.8 per cent are house wife, and 2.2 per cent in house hold service (Table 2.9).

Table 2.9: Job Profile of Respondents in percentage

Job Nature of the Respondent	*Rural*	*Urban*	*Younger Male*	*Younger Female*	*Older Male*	*Older Female*
Retired Class 1	2.2	3.2	–	–	6.4	–
Retired Class 2	4.4	3.2	–	–	10.6	–
Retired Class 3	–	4.2	–	–	14.9	2.2
Retired Class 4	–	–	–	–	–	–
Retired big business	–	1.1	–	–	2.1	–
Retired small business	–	–	–	–	–	–
Working Class 1	–	–	–	–	–	–
Working Class 2	1.1	8.4	10.9	6.5	2.1	–
Working Class 3	–	–	–	–	–	–
Working Class 4	1.1	2.1	2.2	–	4.3	–
Big business	–	9.5	15.2	–	4.3	–
Small business	7.8	4.2	13.0	–	10.6	–
Private job	1.1	3.2	6.5	–	2.1	–
Private job lower level	1.1	5.3	8.7	–	4.3	–
Labour	14.4	1.1	10.9	2.2	10.6	6.5
Cultivator	11.1	8.7	–	–	12.8	–
Housewife	42.2	42.1	–	84.8	–	84.8
Household service	1.1	3.2	–	6.5	–	2.2
Petty Business	1.1	5.2	8.7	–	2.43	–
Unemployed	5.6	3.2	10.9	–	6.4	–

Source: Developed by the author using the data from respondents.

Procedure

The quantitative part of the study using survey method aimed at understanding the nature of intergenerational relations in society.

Table 2.10: Showing Consumption Patterns of Different Socio-economic Group

Consumption	*Urban*			*Rural*		
	Upper Class	*Middle Class*	*Low Class*	*Upper Class*	*Middle Class*	*Low Class*
Air condition	√√					
Car/Tractor	√√	√		√√		
Television	√√	√	√	√√	√	√
Music system	√	√				
Tape/Radio	√	√	√	√√	√	√
Scooter/Motercycle	√√	√		√	√	
Refrizrator	√	√		√	√	
Washing machine	√	√		√	√	
Computer	√	√				
Generator/ Invertors	√√	√		√		
Telephone	√	√		√	√	
Gas	√	√	√	√	√	
Tubule boring	√	√		√	√	
Theresure	√			√	√	
Diesel engine	√	√		√	√	
Bicycle	√	√	√	√	√	√
Animal	√	√		√	√	√
Agriculture land	√	√		√	√	

Source: Developed by the author using the data from respondents.

For this purpose Gorakhpur city was selected as urban location and Reotipur village in Ghazipur district as rural location. In the process of sample selection purposive sampling method was used for urban location and purposive random sampling method was used in rural areas. In urban areas interviewer introduced himself but in rural areas interviewer was introduced by another village member as a research scholar and gave a brief introduction about the purpose of the study. In rural areas and urban poor people, interviewer was mistaken as officials of some governmental agency. This misperception was corrected by explaining to them that survey was purely academic in nature and not affiliated to any NGO or non-governmental organization. They were assured that their responses would remain confidential and by participating in the survey they would not be harmed in any manner. It was also explained that they would not receive any tangible benefits from the study. The interview was started only after establishing adequate rapport with them. Some respondents were illiterate. The survey was conducted personally and in the language most preferred by the respondent, which was Hindi in almost all cases. At first they were asked about the demographic information and after that they were asked to narrate their experiences of intergenerational relations (stressful event to pleasurable events). After this, information on psychological variables was checked on four point scale. If they did not understand any point then it was explained to them through examples. During the course of interview, their understanding of the scale point was checked randomly and confirmed. Approximately two to three or three and half hours were spent in one interview on one individual. After completing the interview the respondents were thanked for their kind cooperation in the study.

Narrative Analysis

Narratives organize a sequence of events into a whole so that the significance of each event can be understood through its relation to that whole. Narratives convey the meaning of events. The simplest definition of narrative, and one that has been traced back to Aristotle in his *Politics*, is that narrative is "a story with a beginning, middle and an end" (Chatman, 1978; Leitech, 1986; Martin, 1986). Labov and Waletzky (1967) stated that narrative provides a method of recapitulating past experiences by matching a verbal sequences of clauses to the sequence of events that actually occurred.

On the basis of these definitions Social Scientist present main three key features of narrative:

(a) Chronological (represent sequences of events).
(b) Meaningful.
(c) Social elements.

Rissman's book, *Divorce Talk* (1990) is a key text which promotes narrative analysis. Cohort analysis (1970) done by National Child Development in Britain provides the opportunity to make explicit the social and cultural context that frames the experiences, behaviour and decisions of Cohort member. In United States, particularly, this emphasis on the importance of understanding individual lives and experiences, as arising out of the interaction between individual agency and historical and cultural context, has become articulated.

Mishler's (1995) framework for understanding the different approaches to narrative analysis is based on what are commonly understood, as the three different functions of language, i.e. meaning, structure and interactional context.

Lieblich *et al.* (1998) suggest that the wide variation in approach to narrative research can be described using two dimension: (i) they examine the content by the form of narratives (What happened and why), and (ii) attempt an holistic analysis which seeks to preserve a narrative, in its entirety and understand it as a complete entity. Whereas 0Labov & Waletzky (1967) republished that narrative is composed of sequence of actions such as a narrative abnormal which may be considered as empty or pointless narrative.

They describe fully formed narratives as having six separate elements: the abstracts, orientation, completing action, evaluation, the resolution and lastly coda.

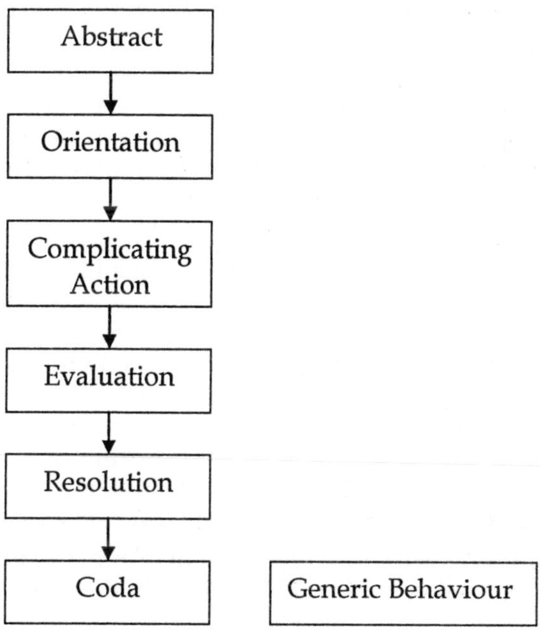

Fig. 2.1: Structure Model of Narrative Analysis (Labov & Waletzky, 1967)

There are six elements of this kind of analysis: Abstracts (a summary of the subject of the narrative), Orientation (time place, situation, participant), Complicating action (what actually happened), the evaluation (the meaning and significance of action), the resolution (what finally happened), Coda (which returns the perspective to the present). On the basis of these elements, they try to understand the structure of narrative and how the elements are functioning and over all process called structure model analysis.

About Analysis

For the analysis I have primarily relied on the Structure Model narrative analysis method which allows an understanding of what process is going on in tandem with an interactive process of data collection and analysis. Structure model analysis begins with finding out what factors influence the situation and how they work, within the research situation. I was trying to find out the lived experience and behavioural pattern of the interacting people in both genders (male and female) by unstructured question pattern related to family life. My task as researcher was to understand which type of relationships the participants experience and what are the psychological factor and processes working between the relations and how these relations affect the well-being. In process of analysis, first of all narratives were abstracted and then the narratives were arranged in a structure. Then I went through the abstracts and arranged the statements in structure told by the respondents in a small form of process. The second step was orientation, i.e. what is the context of experiences or behaviour that the respondents do in combination with what behaviour or action happened then and what happened next. Third step was evaluation i.e. evaluation meaning and significance of the action (what respondent feel or experience). In fourth step, i.e. resolutions, finally what happened, i.e. coping pattern of how the individual handles the situation and cope up with situation. Then, finally Coda was done which means overall which type of relationship they experience.

These overall processes are presented in a tabular form:

Table 2.11: Showing the Way of Data Presentation

Category	Indicator	Priority of older generation	Priority of younger generation	Subjective experiences	Outcome	Coping
→	→	→	→	→	→	→

Category and indicator represent the process of abstraction, and orientation. Priority for older generation and priority of younger generation represents the complicating action. Evaluation covers subjective experiences and subjective experience level covers in outcome (behavioural level), resolution covers the coping pattern, i.e. how control the situation or handle the crisis in relationship. The sociologist have emphasized on one more important issue, i.e. Genre. Genre is broadly defined as a pattern of normative and imagery. Genre can be understood as providing framework that actually or context shared and can, therefore, be used to structure events and experience so that they are meaningful and easily communicated.

Todorov (1990) explains genre function as "horizons of expectations" for reader as models of writings for authors. This study covers horizons of expectations in terms of generic behaviour (for example, which type of expectations one generation have to another).

3

Pattern of Intergenerational Relations in Indian Family*

Introduction

Intergenerational relations studies came to prominence with the emergence of the area of social aging and with the establishment of gerontology as a discipline in the 1940s. The early studies were focused mainly on elderly status in family, the problems of old age and family functions in relation to elderly status.

With the emergence of Intergenerational relations studies, three major approaches were used to understand the phenomena of Intergenerational relations.

Generation Gap: The major objective of the studies was to study the generation gap depending on social and economic changes, and differences in values and attitudes (Manheim, 1952; Eistenstadts, 1956; Davis, 1971).

Across Generation: In this approach, the major emphasis was on perception, in which attitudes of generations towards each other is examined (Brewer, Dull & Lui, 1981).

Intergenerational Relations: This approach came to light in the 1990s, but inquiry began with the establishment of the area of gerontology in 1942 where efforts tried to explain the behavioural and perceptual manifestation of the generation gap. Differences on matter of values, need, lifestyle and attitude are observed between generations and how financial difficulty and parent child

---

* First version of this chapter has been published by *Indian Journal of Gerontology*, Vol. 26, No.3, 2012.

dependency during middle and adult-hood leads to conflict between generations. (Fengler & Wood, 1972; Laursen, Coy, & Collins,1998; Lee *et al.*, 2000). Beside these there are other factors which are also sources of conflict, i.e power, resource, justice and social identity (Sherif & Sherif,1953; Simmel,1950). Other scholars enumerate greater autonomy, independence and personal identity as potential sources of conflict (Laursen, Coy, & Collins,1998; Fuligni,1998; Greenberg & Chain,1996). While still others mark cultural gap like parenting style as the cause of intergenerational conflict (Laursen & Collins, 1994).

Besides, other researchers have also emphasized solidarity in the pattern of intergenerational relations and not only conflict. It was in the mid-1980s that the emphasis shifted to solidarity. Intergenerational solidarity is a fluid concept that one associates to life course events. Intergenerational solidarity refers to positive interaction between generations, to circumstances defined by norms of reciprocity and their acceptance and practice in accordance to individual need and social support/ financial support, complimentary role expectation based relations among family members (Bengtson *et al.*, 2002; Legors, 2002; Merz, 2005).

Robert & Bengtson (1991) explain solidarity on the basis of six elements, i.e. Associational solidarity (Pattern of interaction between family members), Affectual solidarity (positive sentiments held about the member and degree of reciprocity), Consensual solidarity (agreement of values and attitude and belief among family member), Functional solidarity (help and exchange of resources), Normative solidarity (fulfilment of familial obligation, role and responsibility), Structural solidarity (geographical proximity of family member). On the fulfilment of these conditions, generations experience solidarity. Intergenerational solidarity within family includes whole range of domestic, affective and financial service between them.

But in late 1990s, there was again a shift in the emphasis of the studies, as now the belief was that in relationships both solidarity and conflict are integral and that such type of relationship exists and were termed ambivalence type of relationship where both love and hate experiences co-exist. The objective of the study was to understand the complexity of relationship where love and hate both feelings exist (Luscher & Pillmer, 1998). In ambivalent pattern of intergenerational relation manifestation, both the role partners (father and son) have conflicting role expectations, lack of clarity in roles, presence of both positive and negative feelings and such coexisting feelings play a crucial role in determining ambivalence pattern of relationship (Thompson & Holmes, 1996).

Intergenerational Relations in India

In India, Intergenerational relations are represented by the works of Sinha, 1972; Gangrade, 1975; Rath, 1971; where they have tried to understand the phenomena of generation gap with the differences on values and attitudes between generations. Rath (1971) in his study found the older generation to have a positive attitude towards religion and negative attitude towards science whereas for the younger generation it is *vice versa*. The younger and older generations differ significantly on the meaning given to god and religion (Mishra and Prasad, 1978). Younger and older peoples' perceptions towards old age reveal a pre-dominance of negative attitudes and beliefs indicating minority group position for the older people. Though differences were not only in matter of attitudes, other factors like future, financial insecurity, perception of the problem, role activity and status of elderly in the family too lead to conflict in the relationships (Prakash, 1996). Besides, the literature also suggests that if the generations shared values norms and cultural traditions, i.e. (manifestations of shared values and norms). Grandparents provide care to grandchildren in financial constraints, grandmothers help bring up the grand-children, they had higher social adjustment and were willing to take up child care activity, and such elderly who participate in family processes and society experience Solidarity type of relationship and satisfaction (Chaddha & Mongia,1997; Chaddha & Kolt, 2004; Panda, 2004 ; Sonar & Prasad, 2004).

Beside this another aspect of the study is to see the interaction pattern generational relations and role of demographic variable like location (rural/urban), education on Intergenerational relations. In the study of intergenerational support it was found that intergenerational support is less common in urban areas than rural locations. Intergenerational gap was more pronounced in urban families between older and younger generation than in the rural families (Martin, 1990; Mishra & Tiwari; 1980, Bhingradiya

& Kamla,1997). In context of education, Vermani and Sharma (1987) found that younger generation carries negative attitudes towards older generation. These negative attitudes are further strengthened among young generation respondent because they have higher level of education, thus negative attitudes towards the older generation increase with increasing education levels. However, Bhingradiya & Kamala (1997) contend that Education and modernization reduce the intergenerational problem within the rural family.

The existing literature thus shows that the family interaction process, generational role and responsibility are the determinants of the relationship. The role of demographic variables (age: older/ younger; class: high middle and low location: rural/urban; gender: male/female) is still an open question to enquire. Family interaction is guided by the demographic variable. Thus, the objectives of the current study are:

- To identify the influencing factors of Intergenerational relations.
- To see the pattern of Intergenerational relations and role of demographic variable.

Method: As discussed in chapter two.

RESULT

The objectives of study were to identify the influencing factor of intergenerational relations, and to see the pattern of intergenerational relations in reference to demographic variables. After analysing the narratives the issues generations interacted upon were identified. Weather there were similarities or differences in these issues, these were the factors influencing the pattern of intergenerational relations.

Table 3.2 reveals that major proportion of respondents experience solidarity type of intergenerational relations (41.8%) followed by Ambivalence type of relationship (33.4%) and Conflict type of relationship (24.8%). In Solidarity, 23.6 per cent belonged to rural background depicting high solidarity type of intergenerational relations. The percentage of male and female

Table 3.1: Influencing Factor of Intergenerational Relations

Sl. No.	*Categories*	*Operational Definition*
1.	Good	Happy and satisfied with relations.
2.	O.K. (Thik Hai)	Low intensity of Satisfaction.
3.	So-So (Thik hi Hai, Chal raha Hai)	Not satisfied with Relations.
4.	Individualism *vs.* Collectivism	Individualism refers to priority for self and own family (wife, son, daughter etc.) concerns. Collectivism refers to priority given to all family (brother, sister, father-mother, uncle-aunty etc.) members living in the household than to the individual.
5.	Traditional or older values	Pattern of behaviour and values that facilitate the continuity of our customs and rituals, like in-laws following religious norms, showing respect towards older generations, *Ghunghat*, serving soil etc. are included in traditional values.
6.	Daily routines	Pattern of everyday habits associated with sleeping, eating, watching late night T.V., spending free times within or outside home.
7.	Household Work	Refers to daily household activities performed by women, i.e. making breakfast, preparing the school going children etc.
8.	Occupational Preferences	Preference of occupations out of Agriculture, service (government /private) business, profession etc.
9.	Security *vs.* Risk Taking	Security refers to a sense of safety, confidence & freedom from apprehension (i.e. government job is secured). Risk taking refers to a pattern, which may be motivated by need or desire to prove on self (i.e. preferences for private job and business).
10.	Consumption *vs.* Saving	Consumption refers to the act of obtaining and using goods, services, new technology, money and resources for the enhancement of status in the society. Saving of resources for future use.
11.	Child-rearing Practices	The pattern of child-rearing practices adopted by the members in the family like refraining from the use of corporal punishment, teaching the child by the members of the family themselves etc.
12.	Life Style	The general behaviour pattern of individual as expressed in terms of food habits (veg., non-veg., making food with onion and garlic), dress pattern (*sari*, *salwar*, *kurta*) use of cosmetic (soap, detergent, mitti etc), and physical looks (hair cut etc.).

(*Contd.*)

Sl. No.	*Categories*	*Operational Definition*
13.	Appropriate Behaviour	Behaviour that is normatively expected one, like restraining consumption of alcohol in the presence of elders and also not abusing family members outside the house.
14.	Favouritism	Showing biasness towards a particular family member.
15.	Unpredictable Behaviour	Refers to the behaviour that keeps on changing frequently, i.e. change of moods.
16.	Differences in Respect Pattern	Changes in the ways of younger generation of women expressing their respect to their elderly, i.e. use of *ghunghat* (veil of head), daughter in-laws not appearing in front of their father-in-laws traditionally, but now they don't mind to face them.
17.	Education vs. Income	Refers to variations in priority given to the possible pursuit of income or education by both the generations.
18.	Migration	Moving towards urban places in search of jobs and livelihood.
19.	Differences in Role Expectancy	As daughter-in-laws, the older generation experienced greater pressure of expectations from their mother-in-laws. But now the younger generation daughter-in-laws fail to meet even the bare minimum.
20.	Household Skill	To manage the daily household activities, some skills like cleaning the rice, sieving the flour, cooking meals are required specifically for women.
21.	Normative Process	Refers to the preferences of fulfilment or non-fulfilment of filial responsibility, familial norms and obligations. If the generation gives preferences in normative process they experience pleasure in relationship. If the generations experience differences in the preferences at normative processes, then they experience stress and strain in taking the filial responsibility and familial norms.
22.	Obligations	It is a behaviour that is perceived as appropriate within the context of specific personal relationship with kin in the life cycle (*i.e.* care giving and fulfilment of the needs and familial roles).
23.	Support in Relationship	Refers to the preferences or non-preferences of support (economic, emotional and physical) between generations. If they experience the support then their relationship will be pleasurable and fruitful.
24.	Subjective Experience	Refers to the subjectively perceived experience of individuals in their interaction, with the other generations, in terms of loss or gain of power, authority and autonomy.

(Contd.)

Sl. No.	Categories	Operational Definition
25.	Coping Pattern	Deals with the patterns of coping styles adopted in stressful and strain relations in the family between generations. The generations may adopt problem focused (avoid the situation, talk to each other to resolve the pattern and maintain the communication), or emotional focused (avoid the person, block the communication) or Reactionary (Physical and Verbal abuse) pattern of coping mechanisms with the stressful and strain situations. These coping styles will further influence the pattern of intergenerational relations.

from rural background showing such solidarity type of Intergenerational relation are 12.3 per cent and 11.3 per cent respectively. However, among the urban respondents only 18.2 per cent showed solidarity type of intergenerational relations and the male and female proportion was equal at 9.1 per cent. In rural area 6.4 per cent older males and 5.9 per cent younger males have solidarity type of Intergenerational relationship. Whereas in urban area older generation males and females have equal ratio in experience of solidarity type of Intergenerational relationship (4.3%) and younger generation males and females have similar trend (4.8%).

In terms of economic class in rural area, high and low class people shows the solidarity type of intergenerational relationship. Among the high class 3.2 per cent of the respondents from each group, male and female in both older and younger generation, show the solidarity type of relationship. But among the lower class it was found that older male (3.2%) and younger male (2.7%), and among the female older (2.7%) and (2.2%) younger female show the solidarity pattern of relationship. In urban areas, upper class 3.8 per cent male and female from older generation and 4.3 per cent younger male and female show the solidarity. However in Middle class 0.5 per cent respondents from each group older male and older female and younger male and younger female show the solidarity type of relationship.

In Ambivalence 17.7 per cent respondents belong to rural area and 15.7 per cent respondents belong to urban area. In rural area 8.6 per cent respondents are male, 4.3 per cent older and 4.3 per cent younger generation. However, the female proportion was 9.1

Table: 3.2: Patterns of Intergenerational Relations

		Pattern of Intergenerational relations (N)=185											
		Solidarity 41.8%				*Ambivalence 33.4%*				*Conflict 24.8%*			
		Rural 23.6%		*Urban 18.2%*		*Rural 17.7%*		*Urban 15.7%*		*Rural 7.6%*		*Urban 17.2%*	
		Male 12.3%	*Female 11.3%*	*Male 9.1%*	*Female 9.1%*	*Male 8.6%*	*Female 9.1%*	*Male 8.1%*	*Female 7.6%*	*Male 3.2%*	*Female 4.4%*	*Male 8.6%*	*Female 8.6%*
	Older	6.4%	5.9%	4.3%	4.3%	4.3%	4.3%	4.3%	3.8%	1.6%	2.2%	4.3%	4.3%
	Younger	5.9%	5.4%	4.8%	4.8%	4.3%	4.8%	3.8%	3.8%	1.6%	2.2%	4.3%	4.3%
Upper Class	Older	3.2%	3.2%	3.8%	3.8%	—	—	—	—	—	—	—	—
	Younger	3.2%	3.2%	4.3%	4.3%	—	—	—	—	—	—	—	—
Middle Class	Older	—	—	.5%	.5%	3.8%	3.8%	3.8%	3.8%	1.1%	1.1%	—	—
	Younger	—	—	.5%	.5%	3.8%	3.8%	3.8%	3.8%	1.1%	1.1%	—	—
Lower Class	Older	3.2%	2.7%	—	—	.5%	.5%	—	—	.5%	1.1%	4.3%	4.3%
	Younger	2.7%	2.2%	—	—	.5%	1%	—	—	.5%	1.1%	4.3%	4.3%

Source: Developed by the author using the data from respondents.

per cent, 4.3 per cent older generation and 4.8 per cent younger generation. Besides this in urban area 8.1 per cent male, 4.3 per cent older and 3.8 per cent belong to younger generation whereas 7.6 per cent female, 3.8 per cent older and 3.8 per cent younger generation show the ambivalence pattern of intergenerational relations. In terms of economic status most of the respondent belonging to middle class family 3.8 per cent older, younger, male-female both in rural as well as urban location. However, in rural lower class .5 per cent older male, younger male, older female and 1 per cent younger female respondent show the ambivalence pattern of intergenerational relations.

In context of conflict 7.6 per cent respondents from rural background and 17.2 per cent from urban background show the conflict type of relationship. In rural area 3.2 per cent male, 1.6 per cent older and 1.6 per cent younger, whereas 4.4 per cent female, 2.2 per cent older and 2.2 per cent younger generation. In context of economic class 1.1 per cent older male, 1.1 per cent older female, 1.1 per cent younger male and 1.1 per cent younger female are belong to middle class and .5 per cent older male and 5 per cent younger male and 1.1 per cent older female and younger female belong to lower class. However in urban area 8.6 male, 4.3 per cent older and 4.3 per cent younger generations and similar trend were found in context of female and all the urban conflict experience respondent belonging to lower class family.

Main Findings of the Study

- Similarities and differences in values and attitudes, Normative Process (fulfilment of familial obligation, role and responsibility) and functional Process (Support: Physical, Economic and Emotional) and pattern of coping influence the relationship.
- In urban areas, mostly higher class family members experience solidarity, while middle class experience ambivalence and lower class experience conflict. However, in rural areas mostly higher class and lower class families experience solidarity while middle class families experience ambivalence.
- In general older and younger generations and male and female have similar trends in experience of relationship.

DISCUSSION

The present findings reveal, most households experience Solidarity (41.8%), followed by Ambivalence (33.4%) and Conflict (24.86%). The patterns of intergenerational relations vary along class status and location of the family. Most of the urban upper class and rural upper and lower class family manifest solidarity pattern of intergenerational relations. Middle class families, both in rural and urban areas, have shown mostly ambivalent pattern of intergenerational relations. However, the urban lower class family has shown conflict pattern of intergenerational relations.

Pattern of Solidarity

Experienced interdependency as well as fulfilment of familial obligations, reciprocally and extending functional support besides respecting autonomy by both the generations depicts the solidarity pattern of intergenerational relations in urban and rural upper class families. Thus, the study brings into focus facts like emotional interdependence between generations as one of the major contributing factor in promoting interpersonal connectedness and solidarity pattern of intergenerational relations (Koutrelakos, 2004; Phalet & Schonpflug, 2001). The joint families are in the process of becoming nuclear, but functionally through this emotional bond, materialistic interdependency and functional support, fulfilment of familial obligations reciprocally lead to adoptive extended family (Khatri, 1975; Fisek,1995; Merz, 2005).

The rural lower class family are also showing solidarity pattern of intergenerational relations. Most of the families are landless and are dependent on the wage labour which is seasonal and insecure. Thus, some of the members in the lower class family migrate to Gujarat and Bengal in search of manual work, leaving their life partner and their children with their sibling or parents or both. The migrated manual workers' family, till he gets employment, is looked after by their parents and they reciprocate by contributing monetarily regularly to the family. Thus, through the contribution they fulfil the reciprocity of filial obligations in meeting out the basic needs and enhancing the status of family in village community and caste and this leads to satisfactory relationship between generations (Gulati, 1983; Rawat &

Rawat,1986). On the basis of gender there is much homogeneity in the pattern of intergenerational relations within all the three classes along rural and urban residence.

Pattern of Ambivalence

Rural and urban middle class families have manifested ambivalence pattern of intergenerational relations. This ambivalent pattern is also observed on the basis of gender. The ambivalence pattern of intergenerational relations is a consequence of subjective and objective level of fulfilment of reciprocity of family obligations, support and normative process. Though the younger generation objectively fulfils the reciprocity of obligations, support and normative process (fulfilment of familial role and responsibility), the older generation acknowledges their contribution but are not subjectively satisfied with the role performance of younger generation. On the other hand, the older generation wants more authority whereas younger generation is becoming more independent and autonomous and also would like to retain authority in their hands. Though middle class families are satisfied with emotional dependency but they are dissatisfied on the issues of material interdependency values and attitude.

Middle class families are experiencing both functional and emotional dependency but are dissatisfied with the extent of functional support extended to them by the younger generation. Also, the older generation would like to see their children autonomous and independent but they would also like to retain authority in their own hand. Such situations lead to ambivalent pattern of intergenerational relations (Cohler & Geyer, 1982; Kwak, 2003).

Pattern of Conflict

Most of the urban lower class families engage in manual work in the unorganized sector. They manifest conflict pattern of intergenerational relations more significantly than rural lower class families. This pattern of intergenerational relations is rooted in the non-fulfilment of reciprocity of obligations, i.e. though the older generation extends support, the younger generation fails to reciprocate it leading to non-fulfilment of reciprocal obligations in terms of physical, emotional and economic support. Beside this younger generation's non-involvement in work, deviant expenditure on gambling, drinking, substance abuse does not contribute to the subsistence need of the family. However, they expect contribution from the older generation. Thus, this leads to exchange of word (verbal abuse), and to physical violence (Versa-Sanso, 2007).

So, over all in Indian society all the type of relationships exist. Mostly the higher class people and rural lower class people experience solidarity. Whereas middle class people experiencing ambivalence type of relationship and urban lower class people experience the conflict type of relationship. The major reason behind the findings is that in India families function in interdependent model and the generations have emotional and materialistic interdependency. In higher class family generally both the generations are economically independent and they give freedom and autonomy to each other as well as time to time support is also provided to each other whenever required, thus they experience solidarity. However, rural lower class families also fulfil the norms of interdependence through both emotional and materialistic support, so they experience solidarity. On the other hand, middle class generations fulfil the interdependence norms in terms of materialistic support and emotional support, but it is not up to the mark or its does not fulfil the generation's expectation so it leads to dissatisfaction, but due to interdependence they maintain the relationship and feel ambivalence in relationship. Urban lower class families experience economic scarcity in resources which leads to individualistic orientation and they are not able to fulfil the interdependence norms and are not able to support each other which leads to conflict between generations.

In developing agrarian society, intergenerational interdependency is a requisite for family livelihood. The child contributes to the family well-being both while young for example working in the field and contributing to the family economy and later by providing old age security to his her parents. These processes promote solidarity in relationship. But, if children do not contribute in material terms the interdependence of the child is not functional and may even be seen as a threat to the family livelihood. Because independent offspring may take care of his own self-interest rather than the interest of family. These processes, create dissatisfactory relationship and lead to conflict and ambivalence type relationship (Kagtcibasi, 1982b, 2002).

4
Family Dynamics and Psycho-Social Process of Intergenerational Solidarity

INTRODUCTION

Solidarity is fulfilment of complimentary role expectations both in terms of norms and functions between two generations within family. This chapter discusses the Psycho-social Process of Intergenerational Solidarity.

Intergenerational solidarity explains the fulfilment of complementarities of role expectation both in terms of normative (fulfillment of familial obligations, role and responsibility) and functional (economic, physical and emotional support) between generations. Intergenerational solidarity is referred to positive interactions between generations of grandparents, parents and children that counterbalance the ups and downs of life (Legors, 2002). The term solidarity used by Durkhiem (1964) indicated a form of social integration where complementary role speculations are fulfilled and where anomic and egoistic tendencies are disapproved by the society. It means solidarity promotes social integration, by fulfillment of role expectations and support to each other and disapproved the self-centred behaviour and lack of social and moral behaviour.

In the 70s, the term solidarity was used in the context of intergenerational relations with major emphasis on generational conflict and explained that generational conflict may also arise because of cohort-centricism where all events are interpreted by members of cohort in light of their own experiences, values and needs (Riely, Jhonson & Forner, 1972) If these facts prevail, age group consciousness and solidarity may develop (Bengtson. *et al.*,1973; Bengtson & Cutler, 1976). However, McPherson (1983 : 263) identified three processes within family that affect intergenerational solidarity. They are, (i) the expected frequency of interaction between generation; (ii) the similarities in values between generation; and (iii) frequency of helping relation between generation. Presence of these processes in a family would lead to intergenerational solidarity and absence of anyone of these processes will lead to strain and conflict between generations (Bengtson & Black, 1973; Bengtson & Cutler, 1976; Bengtson & Scharder, 1982; Troll, 1980). Intergenerational solidarity among family members includes a collection of shared domestic affection and financial services. The norms associated with reciprocity, the acceptance of such norms by the family members, and their adherence to those norms in accordance to circumstances as per the individual needs, resources or capacity is a significant factor in facilitating solidarity within family and between generations. It is also inclusive as all the members of the family, belonging to different generations are working in the interest of the total family, but not to a single part (Legors and Stassen, 2002 : 258). Whereas, Merz, Schuengel & Schulze (2007) reported that generational solidarity can be identified in terms of support provided by the children to their elderly parents and *vice versa*. Thus, the focus is on reciprocal support. Three types of support are identified. They are: practical support that generations give to each other, in terms of Physical support: helping, caring, financial support and social support. Besides this Roberts & Bengtson (1991) identified six types of solidarity existing between intergenerational solidarity *viz.* (i) Associational Solidarity, (ii) Affectual Solidarity, (iii) Consensual Solidarity, (iv) Functional Solidarity, (v) Normative Solidarity, and (vi) Structural Solidarity. Lowenstein (2002) studied households comprised three generations. He developed various dimensions that emerged from his analysis of data as a central theme that reflects intergenerational solidarity. Seven dimensions emerged from the analysis of data. The dimensions are: (a) division of labour regarding household chores and care of grandchildren (functional and normative solidarity); (b) management of household finances (functional solidarity only); (c) economic and housing issues (functional solidarity only); (d) emotional support and care (affectual solidarity); (e) involvement in the intimate social relationships of other generations (affectual solidarity); (f) space and privacy (normative solidarity); and finally (g) education of grandchildren and transmission of values (normative solidarity). Whereas Daatland & Herlofson (2004) in their work found that simple variants exist and the original Roberts and Bengtson intergenerational solidarity model and dimensions could be reduce to four, implying that solidarity can be expressed in terms of association, affection, functional (helping) and normative (obligation). But, in Indian context Chaddha & Mongia (1997) in their study found solidarity between multiple generations within a family shared values, beliefs, norms and cultural traditions. Promotion of such shared culture reduced marginalization between generations. The stay of multiple generations within a family leads to knowledge about ageing and development of positive attitudes towards old age, thus improving intergenerational relations. Further Chaddha & Malik (2004) conducted study in India and found that four major dimensions like (associational solidarity, consensual solidarity, functional solidarity and normative solidarity) are important in promoting solidarity between generations. Thus, reciprocity between generation in role and responsibilities support and similarities in values and attitude will safeguard intergenerational solidarity.

Literature shows that in the context of Intergenerational solidarity research adopt the family solidarity model develop by the Roberts and Bengtson, 1991 based on U.S. data. However, the family interaction pattern, dynamics of the family and status of the generation in the family, and pattern of intergeneration relations varies from culture to culture like Dottland & Lowenstein (2005) in their study "Intergenerational Solidarity and the Family Welfare State balance" try to explore, is Intergenerational solidarity stronger under the more collectivistic southern family tradition then under the more individualistic northern family tradition? He did a five-country (Norway, Germany, England, Spain, and Israel) comparative study in Europe and found that associational solidarity is highest in Spain, normative solidarity heights in Spain and Israel. Whereas no substantial differences were found between countries as far as functional and affectual solidarity was concerned. Over all Intergenerational solidarity is substantially stronger in southern (collectivistic) then the northern (individualistic).

India belongs to the developing world where collectivistic society is predominant (Sinha, 1984). The Indian values suggest family as the most important social institution and it has remained so since throughout ages. Our nation is known for its documented heritage of stability in family life and the family structure prevalent in India has withstood the ups and downs and happenings across centuries (Sinha, 1984). The Indian family is known for its strong bond between family members, resilience and endurance. In such families father is generally perceived as breadwinner, mother is considered as responsible for the upbringing of the children and also taking care of their needs in the form of love, care and protection. Grandfather has a very important role to play in the family as the custodian of culture and conventions (takes care of the grandchildren in the absence of their parents, and socialize them). Children in the family are expected to respect their elders and provide care for the younger ones and give a helping hand at home when necessary (Pandey, 2007). So, the family members are interdependent and they have materialistic as well as emotional interdependency. It is important to acknowledge that this resilience and strength of the Indian family persists despite being heterogenous and diverse. It is, however, important to point out that although families might be strong and resilient, heterogeneity and diversity characterizes family life in India. There happens to be regional and cultural variations in family structure and functioning. There are variations in the norms and values of family life with respect to religion, case, socio-economic status and pattern of residence (Dhruvarajan, 1988). So, here need to study process of generational solidarity phenomena in Indian cultural context in varied location (rural/urban) and economic class (high, middle and low economic class) and gender (male/female).

Method: As discussed in chapter two.

Result and Interpretation

The result supports three prevalent patterns of intergenerational relations in the society, i.e. solidarity, conflict and ambivalence. A higher proportion of participants experienced solidarity (42.16%) then followed by ambivalence (32.97%) and conflict (24.86%). Higher socio-economic participants experienced greater solidarity. 42.16 per cent (solidarity experience group) comprises 16.2 per

Table 4.1: Process of Intergenerational Solidarity

Category	*Indicator*	*Older generation*	*Younger Generation*	*Subjective Experiences*	*Outcome*	*Coping*
Association al Process	Good	√	√	Younger		Avoid the
	Proper interaction	√		generation is		situation
	Have contact	√	√	experience		
	Change in pattern of	√		Autonomy ,		
	communication		√	independence,		
	Collective decision making	√	√	loss of power and		
	Communication telephonic		√	authority in older		*Continue the*
	Communication face to		√	generation.		*communication*
	face		√			*after some time*
	Lived jointly		√			*all problems will*
	No interference			*Perceived*		*be resolved*
	Family decision taken by	√		*favoritism full*		
	father			*autonomy*		
	Self take family decision					
Affectual Process	Understanding	√	√	Gives		
	Younger did not say any	√		responsibility,		
	thing due to respect			authority,		
	Respect	√	√	autonomy towards		
	Positive sentiments	√		younger. Satisfied		
	Trust	√		with children		
	Closeness	√		behaviour		
	Collective sharing	√				
	Acknowledge the change	√	√	*Father makes*		
	Cooperation		√	*adjustments*		
	Helpful					

(Contd.)

Category	*Indicator*	*Older generation*	*Younger Generation*	*Subjective Experiences*	*Outcome*	*Coping*
Consensual Process	Individualism *vs.* collectivism	Collectivism	Collectivism	Increase autonomy in younger, younger priority to earning due to poverty.	Experience difficulty due to individualism.	Avoid the situation continue the communication, Explain
	Traditional *vs.* modern value	Traditional (ritualistic)	Modernity			
	Education *vs.* job	Education	Job	*Adjustment (inner harmony)*	*Not leading to tension*	*Explain to each other*
	Life style (daily living routine, food habit)	Earlier raiser, not importance to modern facilities	Non-veg., drink, go with arms, show of	*Abuse me due to gun*	More difficulty	
	Differences in household work	Quick response to house holds work.	Saving	*Older have positive attitude towards modernity*	*Clashes & conflict*	Accept the change and adjust with situation
	Consumption *vs.* Saving	Consumption	Risk taking (private job)		Low intensity tension	
	Security *vs.* Risk taking behave	Security (government job)	Go with new technology, business or any job for earn			
	Working approach				*Tension*	Explains communicates with each other
	Differences on view of education	If eligible then go to education	Education foe every body			
	Family environment, Social status		Maintain social status		*Tension*	*Avoid the situation*

(*Contd.*)

Category	*Indicator*	*Older generation*	*Younger Generation*	*Subjective Experiences*	*Outcome*	*Coping*
Functional Process	Economic independency Get support (economic, physical & emotional) Reciprocity Provide support (economic, physical and emotional)	√ √ √	√ √ √ √	Some time problem, if younger generation demand beyond my limit, so I reject it. *Sharing, responsibilities in every area by all family members, love and affection irritated due to our work.* *Dissatisfaction due to scarcity of economic resources*		Adjustment if problem is perceived then talk to each other and they makes adjustment Understands his problem. Accepting After getting employment every thing will be ok.
Normative Process	Fulfills the familial obligations responsibilities Accept the familial role Give authority and responsibility to younger generation Maintain hierarchy	√ √ √	√ √ √ √ √	*Burden* *Dissatisfaction by father duties* *Experience tension due to female conflict*	*Experience tension due to burden* *Tension*	*I think I am wrong, try to correct the wrongs through talk via mother* *Avoid and Accept, Explain and make Communication*
Structural Process	Leave together Have Proximity	√ √	√ √			

(Contd.)

Category	*Indicator*	*Older generation*	*Younger Generation*	*Subjective Experiences*	*Outcome*	*Coping*
	Interdependency	√	√			
Generic behaviour	All the self-preferred values and attitudes and behaviours are expected by other generation. Expected living in joint family, collectivism. Get up timely and pursue studies properly, and care for older people. If not employed then you should look after house work, educate your children, consider about agriculture and buy new property/land. Earn and help us getting your sister married, and save earnings. *All the self-preferred values, attitudes and behaviours are expected by other generation.* *Older should change their mentality, according to the time.* *Earnings should be spent on status symbols like car, a good house etc. Education for all family members, simple life saving for future, should we involve in family decision.*					

Notes: √ represents the similarities between both generations.

In table, *italic and underlined sentences denote experiences of younger generation,* and normal font denotes the experiences of the older generation.

In explanation, *italic shows verbatim of older generations* and the ***bold italic verbatim are experiences of younger generations.***

Source: Developed by the authors using data from respondents.

cent urban higher economic class, 2 per cent middle socio-economic class, 12.8 per cent rural higher economic class, and 11.07 per cent rural lower socio-economic class participants (Table 3.2).

After analysing, the data reveals that solidarity and cohesive type of intergenerational relations are observed as the older generations, who not only fulfil their responsibilities towards family, but they also transfer the authority to the younger generation which in turn fulfils the familial obligations. The physical proximity and fulfilment of complementary role expectations further facilitates and strengthens solidarity type of relationship between older and young generations.

The older and younger generation male differ on priority of values, attitudes, life style, food habit (non-vegetarian, onion and garlic in food), daily routine, allocation of household work and child rearing practices. The older generation subjectively experiences loss of authority and power, but interferes in these issues whenever they feel a need for it. Thus, both the generations experience differences, but manifest solidarity type relationship.

There are also differences on individualism-collectivism, traditional *vs.* modern values, consumption *vs.* saving, status, and security *vs.* risk taking behaviour between generations. Younger generation gives preference to non-vegetarian food, drinking (alcohol) and social status whereas older generations give preference to collectivism, security, consumption and traditional values. Though such differences or similarities are present in both the generations, but their subjective experience vary in terms of tradition *vs.* modernity. Younger and older generations explain (issues) to each other, adjust and maintain harmony between generations. Some older men also indicated positive attitude towards modernity. Besides these both the generations emphasized on collectivism but older generation subjectively experiences increase in autonomy in younger generation and experience difficulties in intergenerational relations. Though both the generations emphasized on collectivism, they experienced problems because each generation has its own definition of collectivism. Individuals shift their priorities and these shifting of priorities create difficulties in relationship but the older generation handles the situation by avoiding or solving the problem.

Older members of the family subjectively experienced loss of power and authority and maintained silence while younger members maintained silence out of respect and affection to the older members in family. Most of the older members of the family conceded that in old age the authority, power, independence and autonomy are transferred to the younger members, whereas younger generation perceived favouritism, shown by older generation to one or another younger member of the family. Both the generations, through fulfilment of complimentary role expectations, develop a pattern of interaction and communication that facilitate cohesive, mutual cooperation and solidarity based intergenerational relations between of male members in the families.

In this section we will try to illustrate the solidarity pattern of intergenerational relations through narratives.

Normative Process: In this context, all the family members live together; fulfil familial roles and responsibilities and feel satisfaction with other generation that promotes affection across the generations. This is the case of an older generation retired government officer. His father was a Sanskrit scholar. The respondent was the youngest of five brothers and lived in a joint family. All the brothers stayed away from their native place due to their far away workplaces but they participated in the rituals or festivals collectively. Besides these both the generations, at times, focus on figuring out the problems, if any. The respondent has five children; all of them were educated and working in their respective workplaces. The respondent lives with his eldest son, who is a civil engineer. The respondent believes that he has given autonomy to their children and administers things in the way they wish.

> ***Illustration 1:*** "He looks after the household responsibilities. For instance, he looked after the whole work and finance of his granddaughter wedding. The children take his advice on the matters of marriage and purchase of property. Earlier, around fifteen years back, on the occasion of eldest son's wedding, he did everything. On the occasion of marriage of other children, he just participated as an observer. His eldest son, according to respondent, understands the responsibilities and fulfils them. Many of my friends tell me that if they do not get their pension then their sons would not care for them, but for me this situation has not arisen."

Younger generation respondent is a civil engineer by profession and the eldest son in the family. He stays with his father. He shares his view as:

> ***Illustration 2:*** "Life is very complicated. By complicated I mean to say that I have been brought up and educated in a very good environment. There were no difficulties. By the grace of God, I was employed at the age of 22-23.The environment in which I lived; all my 7 brothers and sisters (including cousins) lived here. My family scenario is quite big and the social scenario is quite big too. I got married and had children. Afterwards, I felt that the family responsibilities have increased. Apart from the family environment the family background was also such that I kept on doing my duties. Today, also I wake up in the morning and keep on planning these works to be pursued. The work might be familial work, social or job related and sometimes while doing these things tensions do arise. In this process, I get irritated and feel burden and get dissatisfied with father's duties and experience burden, then afterwards, I think whatever I had done was wrong. Then I try to correct my wrong behaviour through talk *via* mother."

These cases explain that both the generations fulfil their roles and responsibilities. Older generation gives responsibilities to younger generation and the younger generation takes and fulfils the responsibilities. At times, the younger generation gets irritated and experiences tension due to the perceived responsibilities as a burden. They cope such conflict situations by avoid the situation and make the communication *via* their mothers.

Functional Process: Both the generations show economic independency, receive emotional and physical support, and live life happily.

Consensual Process: Differences in values and attitudes have been found in intergenerational relationships but the differences are demonstrated through the coping mechanisms adopted to overcome such differences and to facilitate solidarity pattern of intergenerational relationship. For example, the consensual process variables like individualism *vs*. collectivism, traditional *vs*. modern values, life style, consumption *vs*. saving and other below mentioned variables show how the generations perceive differences and cope with that situation, try to make communication, avoid the problem and continue the talk.

Individualism vs. Collectivism: Older generation emphasizes more on collectivism and perceives younger generation family members too collectivistic in terms of priorities of values. However, some old aged family members perceive that younger generations have individualistic value orientation and that led to tensions between generations. Both the generations prefer to avoid such situation of controversy and try to talk/communicate with one another on contentious issues and situations. Older generation people share their views as:

> ***Illurstration 3:*** "In our family, even on, small issues, we all sit together and talk. We sit together, talk, laugh and enjoy."

One more illustration from old generation retired Indian police officer. His elder son is a lawyer and youngest son has M.B.A. and is doing his own business. The respondent's wife has been studied up to intermediate and the two daughters-in-laws are also well educated.

> ***Illurstration 4:*** "We have lived in a joint family and know the importance of joint family. My father died when I was very young. My uncle looked after my education and everything else. It never occurred to me that he was doing a favour but due to increasing responsibilities of children I had to separate from my uncle. Still, we have a very good relation and we help each other. But looking at my two children I am worried. They fight on trivial issues and I do not know what to say."

The youngest son does not contribute to the family expenses and receives favours from the parents. The eldest son looks after the total expenditure of the family and feels annoyed on the favouritism shown by parents towards his younger brother, this leads to tension among siblings and the father maintains silence.

One more illustration from older generation female, she reported that:

> ***Illurstration** 5:* "Today's daughter-in-laws are educated and they think that their mother-in-laws are from old times, but they do not understand that they have more experience than them. We are clear that if there is some loose talk then we will say it straightforwardly. Like, on the issue of separation, I told my son to live separately in the same house. The kitchen is full of all the things needed, so whatever you wish you, can prepare and no one will stop you but live in the same house and do as you desire, no one will interfere. There is no tension and even if there is we continue to live happily."

***Traditional* vs. *Modern Values*:** In the context of traditional and modern values system, the older group, generally, prefers traditional value system and they believe that the younger generation has adopted both traditional as well as modern value system.

> ***Illurstration** 6:* "Look, there is a difference like there is tradition which is of religious set up. Even if there is no change in faith or faith towards God but its practical form can be seen. Look at the Babri Masjid issue. The Hindus who brought it down, they did wore shirts and trousers and did not have any of the so called Brahminical things. We still wear our '*Janeu*'. Children may not follow it but they still maintain that in every ritual the auspicious time and space should be followed by systemically. When they go to village they say that give the *Janeu* or else someone might see us without it. Children have accepted traditions along with the modernity. But there are differences in attitude related to the life style, daily living routine, differences in household work and child rearing practices."

The older generation of female reported that—

> ***Illurstration** 7:* "I have four daughters-in-law and one of them is a doctor. Even today we do not go into kitchen with slippers. When my father-in-law was alive we did not wear slippers in kitchen. Now, we have separate slippers for kitchen. Till my father-in-law was alive I told everyone that do not use garlic or onion in food and do

> not wear slippers in kitchen and my daughter-in-laws accepted it. After the death of my father-in-law I told them if they have to prepare anything with garlic or onion then they can do it by taking the gas stove outside the kitchen. My mother-in-law always interfered and said that cover your head, do not come in front of men of the house, if some elders come than get inside, get into the kitchen only after bathing. I have gone through all this and that is why I gave my daughter-in-laws liberty from all these issues and am adjusting with the daughter-in-laws."

Generally, older generation considers that one should get up early in the morning whereas the younger generation wakes up late in the morning as they sleep late in the night. The older generation experiences difficulties, however, they accept the situation and try to adjust with it.

With respect to the issue of life style, younger generation respondents see the emergence of problems due to differences in food habits.

> ***Illurstration 8:*** "Like, take for example, food habits. We think non-vegetarian food should be cooked at least 2-3 times per week, but father maintains that it should be once in fifteen days. Whatever is done, it should be for a change."

Security *vs.* risk taking behaviour: Older generation in general prefers security while younger generation gives priority to risk taking behaviours. Such differences do not lead to negative consequences for the intergenerational relations as the younger generation enjoys full authority and autonomy from their elders. For example, a younger generation urban respondents is a graduate and has done diploma in electronics. His father was a J.E. in Hydro-electric department. His family has three sisters and wife. Two sisters are married.

> ***Illurstration 9:*** "Nobody is happy with me in the family. Everyone is attracted towards government job and so they are not happy with my business. Government job has its own charm, so parents pressurize me to find a government job

> which in turn leads to tensions between us. I try to be normal and always try to make them understand things but if it does not suffice then what should I do? Father believes that government job provides stability. He thinks that as he had done a government job and earned money and social status, so I should also do the same. But things are different with me. Job security means that you stay wherever you are and you would not go beyond that. Earlier people used to do business with job, but now it is not possible. In today's world, what you do matters, not your place or position."

Consumption and Saving: Older generation generally prefers to save money, rather than using it for daily consumption, while the younger generation prefers consumption over savings, but in this situation they approach problem solving coping approach. Younger female reported that:

> ***Illurstration 10:*** "Yes, there are some differences. Take for example the expenses, we would like to spend more in using oils and gas stove, but they emphasized using less oil, wood, cow dung cobs as fuel to save money. They also expect from us. Earlier people could do with fewer clothes but now there needs more fashionable clothing sarees. My mother-in-law is very nice women but then differences do come. If there is much oil in food preparations then she scolds me. After that we are careful in making things. Earlier I could not understand but now I can see my mistakes."

Attitudinal differences are mostly experienced in the life styles like daily living style, dressing style etc. It has been exemplified below, with daily living style as an example (similar pattern is observed in attitudes):

Daily Living Style: A older generation respondent reported that—

> ***Illurstration 11:*** "Like, my husband eats foods around 8.30 in the evening but the daughter-in-law wants food to be prepared around 10.30 P.M. When elder son advised his wife that mother and father should get food on time, after that you can go out, she understood. On occasions they have

to go out in the evenings also and after coming back no one wants to prepare food, so, they eat outside from hotel. Then after coming home they prepare nothing so it is better that I prepare my own food in time without any help."

In this way, the older generation accepts change and adjusts with changes and shows understanding, co-operative and emotional intergenerational relations in the affectual process. On occasions they experience that the younger generation is not showing respectful and understanding behaviours towards the older generation. This perception causes tension or clashes between generations but the younger generation obeys them authority and of older generation makes adjustments or react some time or try to avoid the situation.

In context of materialistic values the differences are reported mainly in lower class families. A older generation female narrated her stories—

> ***Illurstration 12:*** "There is a lot of difference between today and past. Earlier people used to wear one saree and the other was washed and that was Ok. But now they want different kinds and multiple sarees and then also they keep on demanding."

Apart from materialistic values, there are differences in life style (talking, way of living), differences in role expectancy, fulfilment and differences in work participation. Generally, the older generation perceives differences in life style and control themselves and tries to make their points understood.

Dressing Style: The differences are experienced in terms of dressing sense. The young generation prefers to wear *salwar*-suit whether they are in home or outside, but they perceive that their mother in laws insist on them being properly dressed when they go out. To see off the differences they talk to each other. A younger generation female reported that—

> ***Illurstration 13:*** "In our family our mother-in-law is quite modern as you can see yourself, but sometimes it seems that she is not modern. Like, in our daily routine we wear suits and behave normally, but when we go out like that she feels bad and says that you should not have done that.

We were just adopting the things that you were making us learn like if there is *purdah* system in any home then it is followed. At some places it seems that the generation gap creeps in. There arises a difference between our thoughts. Like we behave as we normally do, not like if some relative comes than we would not come out of kitchen or we do not go out and serve. We feel differences in thoughts there or else otherwise the relations are fine."

Differences in working style like younger generation prefer shortcuts and perceive that older generation takes a long process in doing any job is very elaborate. Younger generation female reported that—

> ***Illurstration 14:*** "The differences between me and my mother-in-law are basically related to the prayer at home which is a bit elaborate. I try to do it the shortcut way. I think it should be done in lesser time as it is related to god only. My mother-in-law is a hard working lady and she continues doing work till late night until the work is completed. She thinks if we do it fast than might be something is done wrongly or incomplete."

There arise no negative effects due to these differences, but the younger generation feels that this mother-in-law should behave like mother. The younger generation also feels that there is difference in the expression of anger and they feel that whatever mother-in-law has to say she should say in front but they feel that they taunt them and make indirect comments. The outcome is generally that they feel pain and to cope up with the situation they avoid it, watch T.V., go out and start talking. Younger generation female reported that—

> ***Illurstration 15:*** "Generally, it happens, like some guests have arrived. It is long back, i.e. it was only a year and half of my marriage and I did not know my mother in law that well and people from my father's home had come. I had prepared something (*pakauri*). I gave it to my husband, my brother-in-law who came in the kitchen, also to father-in-law and in the last I gave it to my mother-in-law. She felt bad that I gave her the dish when everybody had eaten. She thought that even I

> had eaten the dish and had served her at last but the fact was that I had not eaten it. She feels that she is the mother-in-law so she should be served first and than rest of the family. Otherwise, she is very nice, whenever someone comes from my father's home or I have to go out for a function she cooperates fully. But her nature is like that only; she will taunt or say things indirectly. Well if she has to say anything she can say it directly, but she chooses to say it indirectly. Sometimes she will say pinching words about people at my father's home. It pains. Either I cry or sit in the room, watch T.V. or even after that I feel pain than go out."

Attitudes towards inter caste, love marriage. Younger generation female reported her experience with her mother-in-law—

> ***Illurstration 16:*** "My mother-in-law knows (Punjabi businessman wife) me since my childhood (daughter of Sindhi businessman) and our families share long relationship. After graduation my family members started looking for a groom. I used to visit his (husband) house daily and he also used to come to our house as he was my brother's friend. My whole family likes him. But when everyone was looking for my marriage proposals then I talked to him and we went got married in a temple and did not tell to families and were living outside. After three days my husband called up his father and he came and took us home. He said whatever has happened has happened let us go. Mother-in-law told that they might have permitted our marriage, if we shared this with her and says that her family respect has been lowered because of this. She remained unhappy with this marriage, but relations became normal after the birth of granddaughter. But it pains to know that she is unhappy. For now everything is normal."

On the basis of these similarities and differences and on the basis of priorities of values and attitudes, the older generation assigns value to affectual processes and the children hesitate to articulate their feelings because of respect.

The older generation subjectively experiences that the responsibility and authority need to be transferred to the younger generation. The younger generation perceives that older generation makes adjustment and defines intergenerational relations "good, with proper interaction and have contact, change in pattern of communication". On the basis of generic behaviour, it can be concluded that the priorities of values and attitudes among generations differ in terms of collectivism, working properly, no one point its service or business, respect to family to children, should have a routine life (should wake up at time, respect parents). Such differences are leading to subjective experiences of loss of power and authority in older generations. Both the generations adopt problem solving mechanisms to overcome such differences of priorities in consensual, normative and functional process.

Thus, with changing time and space, elderly have changed themselves and have tried to maintain unity in their relations.

Figure 4.1 shows that though both the generations are interdependent, but they differ in terms of values and attitudes (life styles) that generate negative subjective feelings. Besides this, on the normative aspects, both the generation though objectively experience fulfilment of role obligations. However, the younger generation subjectively feels that the older generation is a burden to them. It further reinforces the negative subjective experiences. Such negative subjective experiences lead to stress and strain in intergenerational relations that are coped through problem focused coping approach. Such coping mechanism influences the affectual process positively that strengthens the associational and structural process between generation and contributing to the solidarity pattern of intergenerational relations.

DISCUSSION

As per objective to study the relationships of intergenerational solidarity with different demographic variables, i.e. age, gender economic class and location in Indian family. The study tries to see the process of Intergenerational Solidarity against the background of Solidarity Model (Roberts & Bengtson, 1990). Urban and rural upper class families have experienced interdependency as well as fulfilment of familial obligations reciprocally. Extending functional support besides respecting autonomy by both the generations has contributed in the prevalence of solidarity pattern of intergenerational relations. Thus, the study brings into the

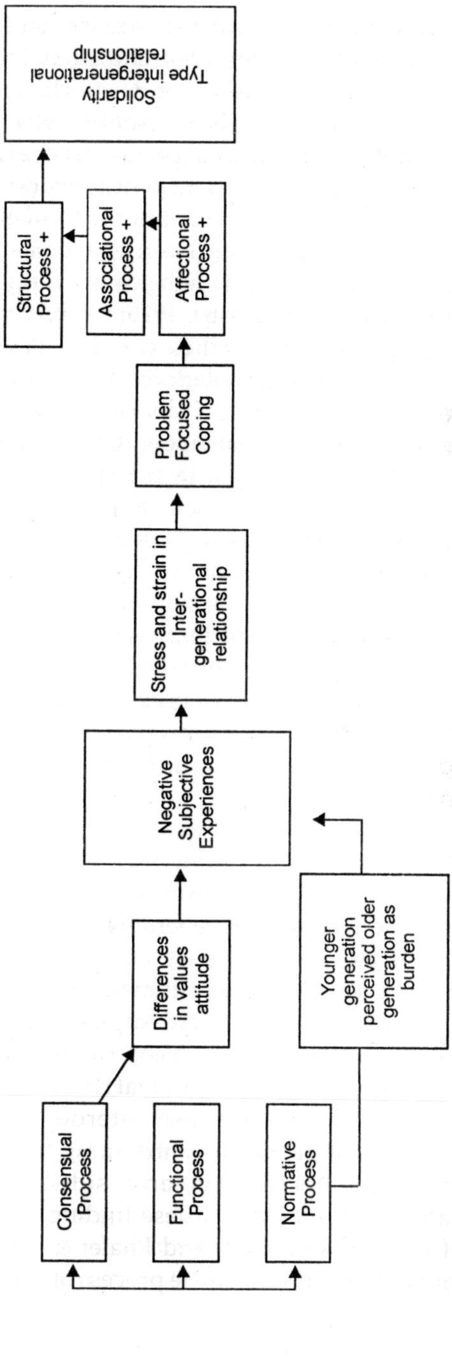

Fig. 4.1: Pictorial Presentation of Process of Intergenerational Solidarity

limelight the fact that emotional interdependence between generations is one of the major contributing factor in promoting interpersonal connectedness and solidarity pattern of intergenerational relations. These findings come closer to the findings of Dekovi, Pels (model in press), Koutrelakos (2004) and Phalet and Schonpflug (2001). The joint families are, may be, in the process of becoming a nuclear, but functionally through this emotional bond and materialistic interdependency and functional support, fulfilment of familial obligations reciprocally lead to adoptive extended family (Khatri, 1975; Fisek,1995).

The rural lower class families are also showing solidarity pattern of intergenerational relations. Most of the families are landless and are dependent on labour which is seasonal and insecure. Thus, some of the members in the lower class families migrate to Gujarat and Bengal in search of manual work and retaining their life partner and their children with their sibling or with their parents or both. The migrated manual workers' family, till the migrant get employment, is looked after by their parents and they reciprocate by contributing monetarily regularly to the family. Thus, through the contribution they fulfil the reciprocity of filial obligations in meeting out the basic needs and enhancing the status of family in village community and caste. On the basis of gender there is much homogeneity in the pattern of intergenerational relations within all the three classes among rural and urban residence.

Findings reveal that urban higher class, rural higher and lower class family experienced the solidarity pattern of relationship. However, there is no difference in experienced solidarity between gender (male and female) and generations (older and younger).

Urban and rural upper class families have experienced interdependency as well as the fulfilments of familial obligations reciprocally. Extending functional support besides respecting autonomy by both the generations contributed in the prevalence of solidarity pattern in intergenerational relations. Thus, the study comes with a fact that emotional interdependence between generations is one of the major contributing factor in promoting interpersonal connectedness and solidarity pattern of intergenerational relationship. These findings are similar to the findings of Koutrelakos (2004) and Phalet & Schonpflug (2001). The joint families are, maybe, in the process of becoming a nuclear but functionally through this emotional bond, materialistic interdependency and functional support, fulfilment of familial obligations reciprocally lead to adoptive extended family (Khatri, 1975; Fisek,1995).

The rural families also show solidarity pattern of intergenerational relations. Most of the families are engaged in agricultural work. Rural agrarian society family functions on the basis of Intergenerational interdependence and this becomes important for the family livelihood. The child contributes to the well-being of family, while being young (working in the field) contributes in family economy and later provides old age security to his/her old age parents (Kagitcibasi, 1982b).

However, the lower class family depends on agriculture labour which is seasonal and insecure. Thus, the youth members in the lower class families migrate to other States (Gujarat and Bengal) in search of manual work and retain their life partner and wards with their sibling or with their parents or both. The migrated manual workers' family, till the migrant gets employment, is looked after by their parents and they reciprocate by contributing monetarily regularly to their families. Thus, through the contribution they fulfil the reciprocity of filial obligations in meeting out the basic needs and enhancing the status of family in village community and caste. Interaction between social units would continue as long as it is profitable for both the role partners and this exchange of support would work in a reciprocal way and facilitate solidarity in social unit (Exchange theory; Merz, 2005).

Figure 5.1 depicts that though both the generations are interdependent, they differ in terms of values and attitudes (life styles). Such differences generate negative subjective feelings between generations. On the normative aspects both the generations, though, objectively experience fulfilment of role obligations, the younger generation subjectively feels that the older generation is a burden on them which reinforces the negative subjective experiences of younger generation towards older generation. These subjective negative experiences would lead to stress and strain in intergenerational relations that are coped through problem focused coping approach to reduce the strain and stress (O'Brieen *et al.*, 1995; Skinner *et al.*, 2003). Such coping mechanism influences the affectual process positively and strengthens the associational process which functions in conjunction to maintain solidarity.

Conclusion

Findings reveal that in urban area higher class and in rural area both higher class and lower class family show the solidarity pattern of intergenerational relations. Both the generations from rural and urban area feel satisfaction in terms of support (economic, social and emotional) and fulfilment of familial role, responsibility and obligations. However, they perceive the differences in terms of values and attitude which lead to the negative subjective experiences. For minimizing the negative-subjective experiences people practice problem focused coping strategies (avoid the problem and continue the communication) and maintain the affection as well as association between generations and experience intergenerational solidarity.

5

Family Functioning and Process of Intergenerational Ambivalences*

Introduction

The present chapter endeavours to comprehend the causes of ambivalent pattern of intergenerational relations in the joint family system of different classes from both rural and urban areas. Intergeneration relation studies have emphasized mostly on the presence and/or absence of solidarity or conflict within the family but these two modes of intergenerational relations fail to capture the complexity of love and hate towards members of different generations in the family (Lüscher, 1998; Lüscher & Pillemer, 1998; Marshall *et al.*, 1993). In order to understand this complexity a new concept intergenerational ambivalence was derived.

Bleuler (1911) was the first person who coined the word ambivalence, later Freud in psycho-analysis applied the term to the situation where the feeling of love and hate exist. The term was latter extended to societal level (Merton & Barber, 1963 : 95) in compatible normative expectation of attitudes and beliefs and behaviour. Individual and society are embedded with status and roles. Ambivalence is more manifested in condition where the role partners have conflicting role expectations. Such ambivalent behaviours are observed among close relationships like father and son. In the context of father-son relationship, father prefers independence of his son from him and simultaneously father resists relinquishing his authority.

---

* First version of the paper has been published in *Journal of Marrige Family & Review,* Vol. No. 49:8, 2013.

Lüscher & Pillemer (1998) identified the ambivalent relation at social structural level in terms of institutions, resources and requirement status, roles and norms and at subjective level through cognition, emotion and motivation.

Thus, uncertainty and lack of clarity may contribute to ambivalent relationship in the family; both positive and negative feelings coexist towards same individual or object. Such coexisting feelings play a crucial role in determining the pattern of intergenerational relations (Thompson & Holmes, 1996). Three aspects may influence ambivalent behaviour/relation between parents and their children. They are: (i) autonomy *vs.* dependency, (ii) conflicting norms, and (iii) solidarity and ambivalence (Lüscher & Pillemer, 1998). The literature of Intergenerational relations and gerontology reveals that the solidarity or conflict pattern of intergenerational relations has received much emphasis (Lüscher & Pillemer, 1998; Marshall *et al.*, 1993). However, the ambivalent pattern of intergenerational relations has received scant attention (Lüscher & Pillemer, 1998). Ambivalent pattern of intergenerational relations manifest contradictory emotions of love and hate, attraction and repulsion, both at the subjective as well as objective levels, simultaneously in pursuance of particular line of action (Weigert,1991). Intergenerational Ambivalence refers to incompatible normative expectation of attitude, beliefs and behaviour. Ambivalence is more manifested in conditions where the role parterres has conflicting role expectations and such ambivalent behaviours are observed among close relationship like father and son. In the context of father-son relationship, father prefers independence of his son from him and simultaneously father resists relinquishing his authority.

Lüscher & Pillemer (1998) identified ambivalent relations at the level of social structure in terms of institutions, resources, status, roles and norms and at subjective level in terms of cognition, emotions and motivations among close relations in the family for instance father and son, where father prefer his son to be independent from him and simultaneously resists relinquishing his authority to his son. Thus, it can be said that both positive as well negative feelings coexist towards the same individual or object or social relations.

Thompson & Holmes (1996) found a lack of clarity and certainty in the aspects of (i) autonomy and dependency, (ii) norms, and (iii) reciprocity and solidarity which may contribute to ambivalent relationship in the family. According to Lüscher & Pillemer (1998) ambivalent pattern of behaviour/relations between parents and their children is a result of the structure of the period (time), status of the parents and the adult child. Specifically, in adulthood, ambivalence exists between the desire of parents for help, support and nurturance from their adult children, while adult children seek freedom from their parent (Cohler, 1983; Cohler & Altergott, 1995; Moss & Moss, 1992). The phenomena of ambivalence as understood as the literature reveals the following process.

Autonomy *vs.* Dependency: It has three major components, like freedom and authority of generation, role allocation (child rearing practices) and autonomy of old generation from the younger ones that determine the ambivalent pattern of relations. People of older generation not only want autonomy from the younger generation but also wish to be dependent on it at the same time. Any threat to the autonomy of older generation leads not only to stress but also results in ambivalence in the interactions between generations.

Conflicting Norms Regarding Intergenerational Relations: Two incompatible norms are observed in the interaction between the younger and older generations. They are the norm of reciprocity which suggests that both profit and loss should be equitable between the role partners, while the second norm of solidarity insists on the extension of help to close family members without concern for a return on investment. For instance George (1986) studied a person providing care to chronically ill old parent. The author observed a long term imbalance in adherence to the norms of reciprocity and solidarity that created personal discomfort leading to the conclusion that one has behaved badly regardless of the strongly adhered norm in the interaction. The care recipients also feel ambivalent as they expect support on the norm of solidarity, but also feel guilty and helpless about their inability to reciprocate. There are also conflicts between loyalty to the chronically ill old parent and their spouse and children, between the demands for solidarity and the desire for reciprocity. Such conflicting norms lead to profound feelings of guilt. Thus, it can be posited that conflicting feelings are based on parent child attachment, socialization factors, competing roles of daughter *versus* wife and mother, solidarity and reciprocity. George (1986) found that adult children perceives more normative conflict as compared to these person who caring towards their children. Adult children forced in to dilemma of when to stop providing care and they often lagged, for the time when rewards were more equally distributed. They also reported conflicts between loyalty to the parent on the one hand, and their spouse and children on the others. Many felt that there was no way to resolve the contradiction between the demands of solidarity and the desire for reciprocity, and they were left with profound feelings of guilt.

So, rather than a simple relationship between the effort of care giving and distress, George in his study documents complex and ambivalent situation, indeed, one can posit conflicting feelings among parent child attachment, socialization factor (gender role, caregiver), competing role (daughter *vs.* wife, and mother) and lastly counter-vailing Social Norms (Solidarity *vs.* reciprocity). George provides compelling evidences in support of normative ambivalence in intergenerational relations. Beside this the phenomena of intergenerational ambivalence is analysed in terms of mixed feelings, attitude and emotions (Pillemer & Lüscher, 2004; Pillemer & Suitor, 2002, 2005) and further he derived that incompatible normative expectation for relationship with children produce contradictory feeling or behaviour and that leads to intergenerational ambivalence. Pillemer *et al.* (2007) in his study capturing the complexity of intergenerational relations, explores ambivalence within later life families and found that parental ambivalence that highlights conflicts between generations on familial norms regarding solidarity with children and expectation that children should become independent. Lower ambivalence was related to an adult child's being married and children problems were positively associated with ambivalence, as was the mother's perception that exchange in the relationship was inequitable in the child's favour. The Mother's perception that she and child share the same values was negatively associated with ambivalence.

So, the basic question is such normative conflict, however, inherent only the care giving relationship or it also apparent in parent child relationship. The major intergenerational work has been done by Western society where independence is predominant. So, where dependence takes place (care-giving) it shows these type of relationship, besides this, in India generally interdependent society exists where the generation are interdependent (physically, emotionally, psychologically and economically) and how this interdependency leads the relationship.

Objective of the study is to understand, how the interaction process between generations lead to ambivalent pattern of intergenerational relationship among the generations, in joint family belonging to different social class.

Method: As discussed in chapter two

Result and Interpretation

After Analysis findings reveals that there is three patterns of intergenerational relations, i.e. Solidarity, Conflict and Ambivalence are exist in society. A higher proportion of participant experience solidarity (42.16%) followed by ambivalence (32.97%) and conflict (24.86%). Further analyse the ambivalence experience group dominated by middle socio-economic group. However, in 32.97 per cent ambivalence experience group .5 per cent participants belong to urban higher economic class and 2.5 per cent participants are belonged to rural lower socio-economic class. This chapter discussion is based on experiences of ambivalence experiencing group-members.

The analysis of narratives reveals that the following major factors like associational, affectual, consensual, functional, normative, and structural processes, also affect the intergenerational interaction. Besides these processes, some factors like values, life style, household work, child rearing practices and coping have also been identified which are played significant role to determine the Intergenerational ambivalence. They are mentioned in detail as below.

The analysis of narratives reveal that changes in terms of power and authority, and differences in normative and consensual process in terms of values and attitudes between generations in the family, may affect the pattern of intergenerational relations. Out of the three patterns of intergenerational relations, solidarity, ambivalent and conflict, the processes that contributed to the emergence of ambivalence type of relationship has been presented in this chapter.

In functional process (Support), the two generations in the family experienced interdependence. It was expressed in financial,

Table 5.1: Process of Intergenerational Ambivalence

Category	*Indicator*	*Older Generation*	*Younger Generation*	*Subjective Experiences*	*Outcome*	*Coping Pattern*
Associa-tional Process	Interaction is ok so-so (not smooth).	√	√	Authority to decision making, some time submissiveness	Stress	*Compromise behaviour*
	Family decision taken by husband.	√	√			
	Family decision taken by father-in-laws.		√	Older generation not live jointly, haply.		
	Clear communication	√	√			
	Lack of communication		√			
	Self-decision.	√	√	Have autonomy.		
	Ok, good.					
	Take decision with consul of children	√				
Affectual Process	Understanding		√	Disrespect, lack of support, indiscipline	Accept Social change	
	Reciprocity in positive	√				
	sentiments among family member	√				
	Distance	√		*Discipline*		
	Respect	√				
	Perceived Social change					
Consensu al Process	Individualism/collectivism	Collectivism	Collectivism (Subunit)	Authority loss, older are rigid	Tension, *Tension*	*Compromise* Daughter in
	Traditional / Modern values	Traditional	Modern (spiritual	Disrespect, Don't tell anybody due	*Ego clashes* Tension, some	law 1stly react then avoid and

Category	*Indicator*	*Older Generation*	*Younger Generation*	*Subjective Experiences*	*Outcome*	*Coping Pattern*
			respect)	to dignity and family status. In earlier time daughter-in-laws go with discipline, respect in present time not these things.	time pain. Some time ok.	accept.
	Differences in life style	Simple & old, normal living standard	Don't change our behaviour live, hi-fi life		*Tension*	*Accept the situation*
	Consumption *vs.* Saving	Saving	Consumption	*Lack of freedom*		
	Child rearing Practices	Don't beat children self teach		Experience differences but not go to tension		Avoid
	Routine activity, differences in work pattern	Make social status	Want sharing, do not delay the work, try to improve & maintain social status.		Stress	
	Differences in view				*Tension*	
	Social status			*Lack of expectation fulfillment*		
	Familial norms	Interdependency, wait elder member for food.	Autonomy	Unhappy feelings	*Tension*	*Avoid go forward*

Category	*Indicator*	*Older Generation*	*Younger Generation*	*Subjective Experiences*	*Outcome*	*Coping Pattern*
	Discipline *vs.* autonomy Unpredictable behaviour	Discipline		We don't understand what is good, what is bad. A short time Ok. And short time period deny	Tension	*Change the behaviour according to in-laws, and request and respect*
Functional Process Physical support Emotional support Economic-al support	Physical and Emotional support Lack of caring and sharing Economic problem	√ √ √		Preferences own families *Lack of Support*	Tension Tension	Avoid, make silence *Avoid, make silence as possible*
Normative Process	Familial obligation Familial role Familial responsibility	√ √ √	√ (some are not) √ √	*Powerlessness* *Lack of sharing responsibility, expectation did not get, fulfilled by daughter-in-laws. The son was a cause of problem*	Pain tension *Pain tension*	Avoid, make adjustment *Avoid*

Category	*Indicator*	*Older Generation*	*Younger Generation*	*Subjective Experiences*	*Outcome*	*Coping Pattern*
				No cooperation in house hold work		
Structural Process	Live together	√	√		Tension	
	No proximity	√				*Avoid*
	Familial dispute	√			*Tension*	
	Make distance		√			
	Some have proximity		√			
	Some do not have proximity		√			
	Have proximity but maintain distance		√			
Generic behaviour	All the self-preferred values and attitude and behaviour are expected by other generation. My all expectation towards my last son. *All the self-preferred values and attitude and behaviour are expected by other generation. We expect that what we do with others, they do the some with us. We want to have good things as we are part of society, while they think that we should save money for future. Emphasis younger go to education, older lift the rigidity and take flexibility and modernity, expected freedom and autonomy.					

Source: Developed by the authors using data from the respondents.

physical and emotional support and support in agricultural work. However, the two generations differed in their perception of support. For instance, older males held that the younger males are not contributing share to agriculture activities and take limited interest in agriculture. It leads to feelings of helplessness among the elderly. The younger members held that agriculture yields lesser returns and therefore, it is not a wise options generation. These differences often result in tensions and conflicts. The participant coped with a strategy of avoiding the person with a hope that in due course of time the issues will get resolved.

Though both the generations respect complementarity of role expectations and responsibilities at a normative level, the older people subjectively perceived that the younger people did not fulfil the family responsibilities and *vice versa*. Such differences lead to unpleasant feelings between generations. For example, one urban middle class male member left his secure teaching job at an intermediate college located far away from his city and became an urban property dealer in his own native place which involves higher risk contrary to the expectations of older generation's emphasis on security of job. This led to unpleasantness in the relationship. Though elders has power to take decisions in family matters, but they feel insecure towards the future of the young generation as they are taking riskier jobs that may not be compatible in fulfilling the normative role expectations on subsequent occasions. Though both the generations live in physical proximity, they maintain a distance of attitude and orientation. The outcome of such situation is stress and strain that's leads to blocking of communication.

In the consensual dimension during familial interaction, people from two generations expressed diverse values and attitudes. For instance, older people perceive that they are losing authority and power as the younger generation is becoming more assertive and showing limited respect to the values held by the older people. The youngsters perceive that the older people interfere in everyday family issues that lead to a perception of curtailed autonomy. In more cases the elders were found to use abusive words for the younger people. This indicated that they are introducing helplessness in the younger people. In this way both the situations lead to irritation, dissatisfaction, and ambivalence in intergenerational relations.

Children are dependent on their parents during childhood while elderly become dependent on their children in old age. This depicts a pattern of interdependency between these two generations. The younger generation aspires to assume autonomy and authority from elderly while the latter want to retain their hold on power and authority. Due to the scarcity of resources and unemployment, youngsters are dependent on the older people while elders claim that they have fulfiled their responsibilities against youngsters. This creates dissatisfaction and ambivalent pattern of intergenerational relations. With a view to deal these situations, people like to avoid the person, make compromises, flow with the situation, show lack of interest in communication, and live together with dissatisfaction in order to resolve the differences. Such coping strategies further promote sustained ambivalent intergenerational relations.

The older and younger generations differ in their lifestyles. Generally, the older people prefer saving and security in life when the younger generation tends to consume more to enhance their status in society and has lesser savings. Such differences are the main sources of contention between generations. To overcome such situations, avoidance/separation/aggressive behaviour and avoiding communication are the adopted coping strategies. Both the generations also differ in terms of values and attitudes.

Let us exemplify the ambivalent pattern of intergenerational relations through case narratives:

Normative Process: In this context the roles and responsibilities are shared at manifested level but at subjective level the two generations perceive in just the opposite way. It leads to stress and strain in intergenerational relations. For instance an older male reports unsatisfactory behaviour of his younger son in the presence of the members of a family that seeks matrimonial alliance of their daughter with his younger son.

> ***Illustration 1:*** "My second son got job as teacher in higher secondary school. Marriage proposals were coming for him, but he preferred love marriage. Although, I did not oppose the idea of love marriage, we had to move according to the norms of society. I called my son in front of the parents of the prospective bride. He came with irritation and uttered "See me, have you seen" and then

went away. At that I felt insulted before the prospective bride's parents. He did not bother about the respect and honour of his family. When the bride's family left, all of us the entire family members including parents, elder brother, sister in law and the younger son) sat together and tried to make him understand the need to conduct according to the norms of the socially approved behaviour before the prospective bride's parents. He was not ready to admit the mistake which led to tension in the family. We stopped talking to each other.

There is also tension in the family due to financial constrains. The eldest son provides financial assistance to the entire joint family. I am a retired employee without pension for the last 18 months. Earlier whenever other members of family were in need of money they used to approach me. Now, my financial condition is weak and I fail to fulfil the need of family members which makes me feel helpless and guilty. It is an additional a cause of tension in the family."

Younger generation female reported that—

Illustration 2: "I cannot weigh my feeling with that of others. What others think about me and what I think about them. I may think very highly of them and do good things, but they may feel bad or hurt or they may think that I feel bad. There are so many assumptions like this. For example. it is a small assumption related to work. I do the work; everyone knows that there is more work in the morning; by noon everyone relaxes. So, if one helps at 10 or 11 am work will be easy, but there is no support. We have small children who have to go to school. Husband also has to leave; father in-law has to leave. It is also important to take bath in the morning. I have to cook, clean the room everything is up when Guest come they have to be taken care of. So on these issues, at times there is tension."

Simultaneously, she focuses on economic problems and says a major problem of staying in joint family is money problem. Like, for example, there is one earning member, running the entire household. When my wishes are not fulfilled I feel that if we were independent or had nuclear family it would have been better.

Functional Process: In this domain, differences are seen in matters of financial and physical support. The members of older and younger generations experience mutual financial dependency and lack of physical support. Differences are experienced in financial investments. The older generation cares for profit and loss and prefers investing more in acquiring land. They feel that the younger generation bothers less about investment. Instead they are more interested in spending money. They expect financial support from the older generation. In this situation, the older generation experiences helplessness. The outcome of such a situation is tension. The participants take recourse to use of emotional focused coping strategies to overcome such tensions. For example, the following case from elderly persons documents his experiences in the following words.

> ***Illustration 3:*** "We got ancestral property, agricultural land, and are maintaining it, keeping in mind the financial security and welfare of children and other considerations. But, the younger generation is not showing keen interest in agriculture. This happens because in early years we had to live in poverty. We have experienced shortage of food. In this age too, we are engaged in agriculture and we know about the profit and loss in cultivation of crops. The younger generation is not mentally prepared to accept cultivation of land as a source of livelihood."

A member of younger generation had another view to share:

> ***Illustration 4:*** "Our family is a joint family (lineal collateral). All the 5 married brothers are employed and live at the respective places of their work. The youngest brother is a petty shop keeper in the village and economically weak, so extend financial support to him. But our father feels think that the youngest brother's financial position is relatively week and he needs more financial help from his elder brothers. This causes tension across generations (father-son). In such situation the father maintains silence for some time. The elder brothers feel that they also have their own families and so we cannot send as much as the youngest brother expects from them, as they have the burden of their own family responsibilities and duties.

The members of younger generation also experience financial crisis due to scarcity of resources. They are not able to extend the physical, economic and emotional support to the older generation. The younger generation gives priority to their wives and children. In such a context the members of older generation perceive that the younger generation tends to ignore the larger family unit. Such perception results in tensions between generations. Thus, the members of older and younger generations experience differences in priorities of values and attitudes. Out of these differences, individualism *vs.* collectivism, security *vs.* risk taking and consumption vs. saving are prominent. They emerged in several narratives as exemplified in several narratives. Let us examine them in some detail.

Individualism* vs. *Collectivism: The members of older generation perceive that they uphold collectivism while the younger generation is giving priority to individualism like the following case from older generation illustrates their point.

> ***Illustration 5:*** "Children are free either to follow the advice or not. I do give my advice but I do not force them to follow it. I take decisions independently and so also the son. Before taking the final decision I think about its consequences and do what I feel as more appropriate."

Another member of older generation male reported:

> ***Illustration 6:*** "Children are engaged in transportation and business. They leave their residence in the morning for work and return in the late evening. At times differences crop up between me and my children on the basis of priority of attention given either to the total joint family or to the respective nuclear family units. The old age male member emphasizes on the priority to the total joint family. On this issue the children used to oppose me. In such circumstances, the elderly males make compromises and convince themselves that the children are mature enough and have autonomy in making their own decisions as long as they are carrying out the responsibility of the parents. The elders view that children allocated responsibilities and through this will bring in parental control. I feel that if I

> tell all the children to earn and run the house then I would facilitate the fulfilment of their own family unit's interest."

Traditional and Modern Values: Both generations differ in values. Younger generation prefer modern value and does not bring any change in their behaviour. They show respect in spiritual way while older generation prefer traditional value and accept it. Change in behaviour and respect is shown in physical way. On the basis of these differences, they subjectively experience lack of freedom and in outcome tension is perceived. To cope up with it they accept the situation. Older generation female reported that—

> ***Illustration 7:*** "She is high school educated and her husband is retired, she has five sons, and daughter-in-laws who all are graduates. She reports. "In our times we used to go veiled, in front of our elder rather we tried to avoid going in front of them. Today's women are not bothered about who is where. I told my daughter-in-law that if you have to wear suit you can wear it at home but when you go out wear *sari*. On this she replied time has changed. It seems that let them do what they want. I remain quiet. In older generation times unless elders had eaten we did not eat. Now-a-days, women eat irrespective of whether anyone has eaten or not. When I try to make them understand they either do not listen or argue."

Younger generation in her family members include husband, father-in-law, and mother-in-law. Mother in law is a 6th standard pass and she is doing Ph.D. in English literature she reports:

> ***Illustration 8:*** "There is a difference in the way they dress up. They wear *shalwar-kameez*. There is no veil and they do not cover their head. She keeps on saying like this I have experienced that, but I have not changed and maybe, that's why others have changed their views. This view point was more of outsiders than the family members due to which I did not feel hurt and tensed and because the family members were with me, therefore, there was hardly any problem. We are not able adjust with those views/ thoughts, like this should not happen they give importance

> to auspicious and inauspicious rituals. They want physical respect rather than spiritual. If someone respects them from heart/internally they do not acknowledge it or give any importance. This is the basic difference. My family is rigid. On this day or that day that should be done. I do not believe in it and thus there is tension because my mother-in-law has faith in it so I have to do that."

Apart from values, difference in attitudes is also reflected i.e. difference in life style, consumption *vs.* saving, child rearing practices and routine activity work pattern of families. On these older generation often gives emphasis/importance to normal loving standard and want to live in its real standard and emphasizes on consumption due to this they experience subjectively less of authority and blame education. The outcome is tension and conflict and to cope up with this they maintain a silence and stop communication.

Security* vs. *Risk Taking Behaviour: Older generations generally prefer government job as it provides more security and stability to life. The younger generation prefers private jobs as greater incentives are available. These differences in priority of values make intergenerational relations strained. The following excerpt from the narrating of a member of older generation illustrates it.

> ***Illustration 9:*** "I can not understand the children's ways of thinking. The future is not bright if they continue what they are doing and they want to do. I do not have any job security. I want that he should take up some serious job or business, but he wants to join politics. This has become source of conflict. The elder son qualified in written examination of APO (Assistant Prosecuting Officer), but failed in the interview. Then he joined as lecturer in school and worked for few days. After that he left the job. A heated argument took place between me and aim. I stopped talking with him. My son preferred to take his own decision independently, and I left the decision to him. My son says the world has changed a lot and one should move with the changing world. He pleads that the job of lecturer does not go with his aspiration as it will lead to stagnation after sometime."

The son a member of younger generation reported as follows:

> ***Illustration 10:*** "Daddy is angry/upset with me because I left the lecturer's job after working for three months. I started my own business and am trying to enter into politics, which my father does not like. We had differences in our views and therefore, I withdraw from interacting with him. After this incident, there emerged stress and strain in our relations. Both of us sat down and tried to sort out the differences. My view was that earning money is more important than the means. My father said that this type of earning is not stable and so the means are more important than the ends."

Consumption* vs. *Saving: This issue was reflected in the following excerpt from a person of older generation:

> ***Illustration 11:*** "I believe in saving money and spending it wisely. For instance, I had a Maruti 800 (2000 model), I do not need another car. The son bought another car for Rs. 5 lakhs without seeking my advice and informed me three months later through his mother which led to a minor conflict. After a couple of days I controlled myself and thought that the money spent on car was earned by the son himself and there is no need to get upset."

The younger generation often experiences stress when the older generation compares the living pattern and eating habits of their time with the present ones and expects the younger generation to follow the same pattern. To cope with this situation, the younger generation avoids not only such situations, but also stops communication. Thus, interaction resumes between the older and younger generation after some time. The same is apparent in the following example from a younger generation:

> ***Illustration 12:*** "When we buy clothes, parents used to say that in their days they used to get away with a pair of pant, shirt, what is the use of buying so many expensive clothes? This difference leads to tensions."
> "My father always says that in his time he got job at the

age of 22. He is always cribbing that everyone has now become useless. He says that during his time, they used to get job despite having less education, what is the use of such high education."

Older generation Female narrated her story—

Illustration 13: "She is intermediate and daughter-in-law is post-graduate, her husband is class two employee in telecom and son is in private job. She reports: "we think that it is better to save some money and we do so. We think that only god knows what the next generation would do. But these people think less." Children spend recklessly like we have scooter we say that we should manage with it. There are just two people but they say that mummy having a car is a different thing. Then I made her understand that the son does not have a stable job, you must save money."

The older generation compares their food habits with their children and also in the manners to shows respect pattern. This illustrated with the following excerpt from old generation respondent.

Illustration 14: "Differences in eating habits are quite visible. The vegetarian food milk and ghee were important. Now, these things have been replaced by egg, fish and mutton. People have started giving importance to the non-vegetarian food items. These differences create the stressful situation, in this situation we avoid talking to the younger generation and adjusting with situation."
"We respected the elders whether he was stupid or foolish, or capable or incapable of doing things. Now, I am witnessing that with a little bit of education the son tells his father "you are a fool", you donot know anything. I could not say this even to my elder brother, the behaviour of younger generation upset us and we avoid communications with them."

In such situations, the emotion focus strategy is adopted to cope. This includes avoiding the person, blocking the communication, and going with the situation.

In general differences in terms of expectations of values, attitudes and normative and functional processes between generations were present. The members of older generation felt loss of authority, power, lack of respect and loneliness. The younger generation is looking towards future security. The younger generation seems to ignore the older generation. Though the younger generation tries to fulfil the complimentarity of role expectations the subjective perceptions result in ambivalent pattern of intergenerational relations and are coped mostly through emotion focused approach, i.e. avoiding the person or delaying communication or to go with the situation with a continuity of dissatisfaction and stress in intergenerational relations.

Figure 5.1 is based on the experiences of 29.70 per cent middle class, 2.5 per cent lower class and .5 per cent upper class people who are experiencing ambivalence in relationships. Figure 5.1 shows that while generations differ in consensual and normative processes as far as values and life styles are concerned the roles and obligations complimentarily, but functionally both the generations extend physical, emotional and economic support to each others. Lack of confrontation has also been showed by younger generation in decision-making with respect to the issues of investment and saving. The older generations subjectively feels loss of power and authority such subjective feelings, loss of power and authority result in negative experiences and later to stress and strain in intergenerational relations. These stresses and strains are coped through emotion focused mechanism that simultaneously develops the pattern of love and hate in affectional process. The associational and structural processes continue to contribute positively to the continuity of intergenerational relations. Maintenance of love and hate pattern in affectual processes in intergenerational relations results in the development of ambivalent pattern of intergenerational relations.

DISCUSSION

The middle class families manifest an ambivalent pattern of intergenerational relations. This was a consequence of discrepancy in the objective fulfilment of family obligations, support provision and normative process by one generation and subjective perception as "inappropriate" by the other generation. It was found that the

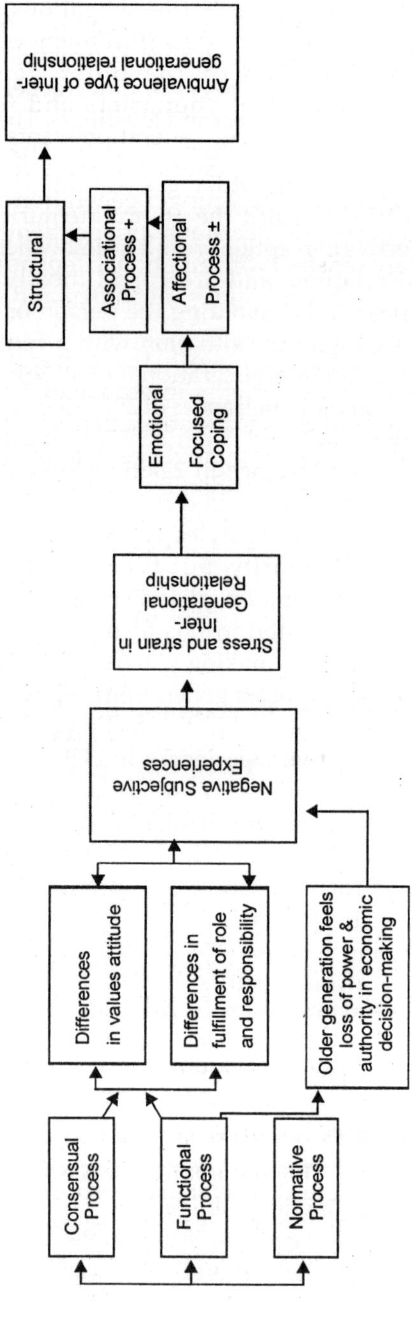

Fig. 5.1: Pictorial Presentation of Process of Ambivalence in Intergenerational Relationship

younger generation objectively fulfils the obligations, extends support and abides the normative process (fulfilment of familial role and responsibility). Though the older generation acknowledges the contribution of youngsters and feels less satisfied. On the other hand, the older generation wants to retain authority where as the younger generation tries to become independent and autonomous. The younger generation also likes to take financial and economic decisions independently. These middle class families are satisfied with emotional dependency and dissatisfied with differences in values, attitudes and material interdependency.

In the middle class families, both the generations are experiencing functional and emotional interdependency. At the same time, the older generation felts dissatisfaction with the extent of support extended to them by the younger generation. The older generation, on the one hand, expects that their children may have autonomy and independence, but still likes to retain authority in their own hand. Such situations result in the emergence of ambivalent pattern of intergenerational relations. It has been observed in the USA (Cohler & Geyer, 1982; Kwak, 2003). However, in a developing country like India, ambivalent pattern of intergenerational relations have been noticed profoundly across the rural as well as urban middle class families. It denotes the coexistence of solidarity and inherent sustained tensions between the two generations. For example, a father teaches his wards to be independent, but, at the same time, he does not show any interest in relinquishing the authority (Mittness, 1991, as cited in Lüscher & Pillemer, 1998 : 418). The state of ambivalence provides as apace for some dissatisfaction in relationships between these two generations, but still they prefer to stay as well as support each other. So, they feel pain as well as pleasure in their relationships.

Figure 5.1 indicates that both the generations assign differential importance to consensual and normative processes in terms of value preferences and life styles. Functionally, both the generations extend physical, emotional and economic support to each other. However, the youngsters do not discuss their plans of investment and saving with elders. Such situation results in subjective feelings such as loss of power and authority related to economic decisions. The subjective feeling of loss of power leads to negative experience in the older generation and later converts into stress and strain in intergenerational relations. These adverse situations are coped through emotion focused mechanisms that lead to affectional processes, where love and hate coexist. Thus, the associational and structural processes continued to contribute positively to intergenerational integration, but the coexistence of love and hatred resulted in the development of an ambivalent pattern.

Conclusion

The study was intended to assess the process of intergenerational ambivalence in the social context with the demographic variations. The findings reveal that the middle class families advocate as well as practice ambivalent pattern of intergenerational relations across the urban and rural families. In middle class families, both the generations, from rural and urban get satisfaction with respect to economic, social and emotional support. But, in terms of fulfilment of familial role, responsibility and obligations, they perceive the differences. The younger generation perceive themselves up to the mark regarding fulfilling the responsibility, but the elders have second version. The elders find the younger incompetent and inappropriate. As a result, both the generations develop negative subjective experience. It can be seen that for minimizing such negative subjective experiences, both generations people use emotion focused coping strategies such as avoiding the person, blocking the communication and flowing with the situation. Along with, they also maintain the affection (love and hatred) and association which perpetuate the ambivalent pattern of intergenerational relations.

6
Family Dynamics and Process of Intergenerational Conflict

Introduction

This approach was introduced in the 1990s, however, the research endeavours in this direction began when the area of gerontology came into being in 1942 where the behaviours and perceptions with respect to generation gap was explored. Scholarly attention was directed towards differential values, needs, life styles and attitudes of the members of different generations. The economic strains and parent child dependencies during middle adulthood was also explored as possible causes of conflict between generations (Fengler & Wood, 1972; Stenman, 1979; Arnctt,1999; Lausen, Coy & Collins,1998; Gimchung, 2001; Lee *et al.*, 2000). Apart from these, other factors like power, resource, justice and social identity were also investigated as sources of conflict (Sherif & Sherif, 1953; Simmel,1950; Austein,1979; Tajfel & Turner,1979). Whereas, other scholars have added factors like greater autonomy, independence and personal identity as potential sources of conflict (Laursen, Coy & Collins, 1998; Collins & Russell, 1991; Fuligni, 1998; Greenberg & Chain, 1996).

Differences on matters of values, needs and life styles are observed between generations and such differences lead to conflicts between generations. This can be termed as an intergenerational conflict. If conflict arises within the family it is more likely to occur between parent and children during the critical years of identity formation and independent assertion.

Sometimes, intergenerational conflicts may result in the

formation of age homogeneous political or social groups at macro-level seeking change or stability in society.

Cohen & Ganes (1978) argued that socialization involves two ways process of interaction, negotiation and interpretation of meanings. On the basis of negotiation and meanings either cohesiveness or conflict between generations will emerge within families. Bengtson & Kuypers (1971) found that older generation has an interest in the *status quo* and in the maintenance and continuity of those values that were considered as salient to them. Therefore, they seek to inculcate similar values in younger generation. Younger people seek to develop a life style and unique set of values that are different from the older generation and promote differences between the generations. Such intergenerational differences in values and life style may be perceived as a source of intergenerational conflict.

Fengler & Wood (1972) studied value differences in families continuing three generation controlling variables like gender, education, religion and place of residence. They found that age difference resulted in generational differences in values and attitudes. Bengtson, Furlong & Laufer (1974) disagreed with the age based differences on similarity or intergenerational differences.

Stenman (1979) examined the parent and child conflict during adulthood in U.S. in three generational families. He suggested that crisis in the family like illness, death of one parent, financial difficulties for the elderly person, or a divorce or financial crisis on the part of the offspring can increase parent child dependency during middle adulthood. These crises can result in three types of the intergenerational conflicts in the family:

1. *Continuing Conflict*: The underlying tension of the crisis in middle adulthood will always exists in relation to meaning of life, values, morals, friends or religion;
2. *New Conflicts*: In which Parents and adult children disagree on their respective roles of caring the surviving parents or rising the third generation; and
3. *Unresolved Conflict*: In childhood conflict may reappear with renewed or increased interaction between parents and adult child.

In aging society, the aged members will experience a loss of political power as this power will shift towards older adults, due to their considerable and still progressing as their voting power that would make them appealing to politicians and power brokers. This can prove as a significant reason for open conflict between younger and older generations more than covert prejudice or stereotypes against elderly (Butler, 1969). There is a greater increase in intergenerational conflict between parents and children at the advent of adolescence and is usually at its peak. However, it gradually declines by late adolescence and young adulthood. This variation can be attributed to the establishment of greater autonomy and independence, development of own personal identities, adoption of value system and fostering social relationships with individuals other than parents. The transition from family home to college may lead to loosening of parental control and can contribute to the decrease in family conflict (Arnett,1999; Laursen, Coy & Collins, 1998). Laursen *et al.* (1998) argued that the majority of empirical researches on intergenerational relations in family were conducted mostly on European and American population, neglecting the role of cultural factors in the development of intergenerational conflicts and their management.

Laursen & Collins (1994) reveal that intergenerational conflict in family generally occurs during adolescence over issue of autonomy and independence. The children emphasize on Western individualistic values, attitude, life styles, while the elderly gives priority to collectivistic values. Such differences in value are a source of conflict between generations within family. These cultural differences between parents and children get accentuated when the children join college. It further results in greater misunderstanding and conflict between generations, (Lee, Choe, Kim & Nago, 2000). Contrasting values such as that of individualism and collectivism also can result in hurtful exchanges and conflicts between parents and young adults (Zhou & Bankston, 1998).

Children who assert more on their autonomy and independence experience frequent intergenerational conflict in family and less cohesion with their parents (Collins & Russell, 1991; Fuligni, 1998; Greenberg & Chain, 1996; Gold, 1989). Seelbach & Die (1988) in their study found that families in multiple generations reside under the same roof, is more likely to increase stress and conflict due to the frustration that arises from the situations in parental egocentrism encounters adolescent egocentrism and often results in alienation and segregation. In such situations, despite co-residence, there is little mutual understanding among family members. This further gets intensified in the absence of fluency in a common language, further intensifying alienation and segregation with little hope to counter the ever widening gulf (Lee & Cynn, 1991). So, after changing social world and situations generation face differences in values and attitude and feel crises due to perceived differences in terms of autonomy *vs.* dependency, which leads to stress and strain in relationship. This chapter tries to explore the family dynamics, differences in values and attitude, what are the behavioural manifestations generations shows during differences and what are psychological process adopt during differences in behaviour.

Method: As discussed in chapter two.

Result and Interpretations

The result supports three prevalent patterns of intergenerational relations in the society, i.e. solidarity, conflict and ambivalence. A higher proportion of participants experienced solidarity (42.16%) then followed by ambivalence (32.97%) and conflict (24.86%). Out of 24.86 per cent conflict experiencing group 17.6 per cent respondent belongs to urban lower class, however, 4.4 per cent respondent belongs to rural middle class and 3.2 per cent respondent belong to rural lower class.

Table 6.1 reveals that lower class urban families predominaly have dissatisfying and conflict pattern of intergenerational relations between older generation and younger generation of male members within family. However, in one urban middle class family and a lower class rural family also manifested conflicting pattern of intergenerational relations between male members. Though the older generations fulfil objectively their responsibilities towards younger generation in functional process like physical, emotional and economic but younger generation provides only emotional support. But both the generation subjectively perceive that the responsibilities are not fulfilled. Besides this, the younger generation is more individualistic in this orientation respective of their physical proximity or distance.

Table 6.1: Process of Intergenerational Conflict

Category	*Indicator*	*Older Generation*	*Younger Generation*	*Subjective Experiences*	*Outcome*	*Coping Pattern*
Associational Process	Not good	√	√			
	OK, (but Painful)	√	√			
	Individual decision making	√	√			
			√			
	Collective decision making		√			
	Not satisfied					
Affectual Process	Did not feel happy with next generation	√		Authority loss Due to crisis want separation		
	Closeness some time before after some time disrespect	√				
	Differences in behaviour	√	√	*Verbal abuses due to crisis*	Tension	
	Distrust	√	√			
	Acknowledges social change	√				
	No communication		√			
Consensual Process	Individualism *vs.* Collectivism	Individualism	Individualism (after marriage)	*Give priority to younger son, individualism and perceived liability as a burden* Physically abused his	Tension *pain, negative behaviour consequences, high level of dissatisfaction*	Used to, silent Avoidance

(Contd.)

Category	Indicator	Older Generation	Younger Generation	Subjective Experiences	Outcome	Coping Pattern
	Differences in life style		Attach to priority to alcoholic drink	mother, *Exercising power*, verbal abuses	Tension	Some time physical fighting
	Differences in earning approach	Do hard work, do some thing, don't sit without work	Private job, continuously changes the job	Negative behaviour consequences *Interference*	Tension,	*Stops the communication*
	Social status	Managing social status		To maintain social status take debt	*Tension*	
Functional Process	Everybody has their own income	√	Priority to own family	In earlier times we took care of our elderly but in present time we are caring the younger generation also.	Pain, fight, conflict tension	Avoidance, blocks the communication
	Physical support	√		Feeling insecurity.	*Tension*	*Blocks the communication*
	Emotional support	√		*Preferences generations to one's priority, older generation abuses verbally, younger generation depended on older generation.*		
	Economical support		√		Conflict	*Accepts due to father's illness.*
	Economic crisis	√		Experience problem due to poverty Family exploitation due to sharing Income	Tension	
Normative	Dissatisfaction with	√		I don't want to see in	Tension and	Left the situation

Category	*Indicator*	*Older Generation*	*Younger Generation*	*Subjective Experiences*	*Outcome*	*Coping Pattern*
Process	familial role Did not fulfil the role Dissatisfaction with familial responsibility We fulfil the responsibility Accept the role Did not fulfil the obligation	 √ √ √ √	 √ √	the family Blaming for his children's death	conflict High intensity of tension, *Tension, pain*	Sometimes abuses, Aggressive behaviour towards younger generation, Blocks the communication *Some time avoid the person, Acceptance*
Structural Process	Live together Some are separate No proximity in physical level Residential propinquity of family members Make distance Poor health	√ √ √ √	√ √ √ √	 Tension *Perceives father as mentally ill*		
Generic behaviour	*All the self-preferred values, attitudes and behaviours are expected by other generation. Doing work properly, earn through hard work, feel responsibility. Children should not rebel. **All the self-preferred values and attitude and behaviour are expected by other generation.* *Provides money for business, don't give importance to one, should arrange for four children if thee are four.* *Expected economic support for business, we want the work to be done appropriately.*					

Source: Developed by the authors using the data from the respondents.

Both the generations differ in their perception of values and attitudes as observed individualism and collectivism, life style, work pattern, child rearing practices and social status maintenance, differences in such values and attitudes are manifested through verbal and physical abuses and conflicts in the intergenerational relations.

Both the generations experience scarcity of resources for survival in terms of finances and expect the other generation to share and fulfil the familial obligations. However, both generations behave indecently. They donot share income and other family responsibilities. These differences are leading to stresses and the older generations do not want to see the tensions and conflicts in the family so they stop the communicating with each other. Most of the older generation members concede to the fact that in old age they have to encounter authority loss, disrespect, distrust, and are not happy with the behaviour of their younger generation. These differences are prompting younger generation to separate (due to economic crisis) from their parents. On the basis of these differences both generations feel that the relationship is ok, but feels dissatisfied with individual level decision-making process.

In this section we will try to illustrate the conflict pattern of intergenerational relations through narratives

Normative Process: In normative process generally both the generations perceive that they fulfil their roles and responsibilities, but the other generation perceives just opposite. It is leading to stress and strain in intergenerational relationship. For example a Class 4th government employee in Nagar Nigam, his wife is a house hold servant. His two sons are employed as private car driver. The older male reports:

> ***Illustration 1:***. "There is a major difference in the way our children think/see things. The younger generation today, does not feel responsible. They just want ready food. They are not bothered to work hard. Earlier, we used to take care of the aged and elderly (*purania*), but now-a-days, besides taking care of ourselves, we have to look after the younger generation too. I doubt what the younger generation of today will do for us."

The older generations feels that in their youth they used to take care of the elderly and at present have to look after not only themselves but also the present younger generation. The younger generation wants to live separately, keep their earnings income to themselves and desires that the older generation people should pass their property to the younger generation. In the entire narrative, there is a feeling of insecurity due to which there is pain, fights, tension, conflict between older generation and younger generation.

Functional Process: Generally, older generation perceives that the younger generation is dependent on them as the younger generation does not fulfil their duties to the older generations. Besides this they do perceive extension of support from the older generation to them. Older generation reports that.

> ***Illustration 2:*** "Son (*chora*) was a driver and never used to give a single penny for the house. He kept the money to himself and contributed Rs. 10,000 at the time of my Daughter's wedding. After six months, I thought of building a two-room flat/house for which I asked him for money, but he refused. Four months after this event he gave me Rs. 35,000 for his own wedding and when I asked he said nothing. I was so hurt by such behaviour, on the part of children that I organized and arranged for the entire wedding only with the amount that he gave and did not even spend a single penny of mine."

In another case younger generation respondent, he is private driver and his father is a government employee, reports that—

> ***Illustration 3:*** "I earn Rs. 2000 per month and with this money only, I have to cater to the need of my wife and children. On being asked for money by parents, I tell them that firstly I will keep aside a portion of savings for them (wife and children) and then only I would be able to contribute to the needs of the parents. They start calling me names. My temper flares up and I also say something, as a result tension erupts. After that incidents neither I initiate talks with them nor they incite."

In another case younger generation report that—

Illustration 4: "Eldest son lives on seasonal employment and remains most of the year unemployed. His father, an agricultural labour, owns a goat (*Khassi*) which he does not want to sell. Then the eldest son sought the money received after the selling of the goat (*Khassi*) from his father in order to purchase trolley (*Thela*) and start working throughout the year. His father had asked his son to make his own arrangements. The eldest son has two children along his wife. Such responses lead to tensions and conflicts between older generation and younger generation.

Functional process makes it clear that generally both generations experience scarcity of economic resources in the family and are dependent on one other. But the older generations subjectively feels that the younger generation is individualistically oriented and not extending support to them, but savings their incomes. The older generation feels insecurity, experiences problem due to poverty and family exploitation, and saving income by younger generation. Whereas younger generation prefers their priority and experience abuse by older generation due to dependency towards older generation and the outcome is pain, tension, conflict, fight. To cope up with this situation they avoid the person and block the communication.

Besides the functional and normative process the both generation experiences differences in attitude and values. In values major difference lies in:

Individualism and Collectivism: The older generation and younger generation differentially emphasis on collectivism and individualism. Older generation male reported that—

Illustration 5: "I have three sons. Only the eldest son is married. I am fulfilling responsibilities of the all three sons. Eldest son has been helping me since he started the work, he only was the owner/proprietor. He was engaged in unfair dealing/unfair money transactions. Now, the one generation younger son to him has also joined him/has also started working along with him, he is having problems. He wants that I arrange for a separate and an independent business set up for the younger generation son. As I do not want, he wants; he gets drunk and starts abusing."

Younger generation reported that—

Illustration 6: "We were separated recently. Our way of thinking also differs radically. They think that he is elder. For instance I do not own a house (there is a room and a verandah in the house). The younger generation has been married, he would also have to stay in that house only, so now you vacate and leave. Recently, it so happened that there is a verandah, room, at the backside of the house. Earlier we used to live there. Younger generation brother's wife has come to stay at our house. I thought that first we make arrangements and then this ceremony (*gowna*) be held. Father asked me to stay elsewhere outside as it was a matter of 10-15 days, he would make alternate arrangements afterwards. They started living inside and we came out. No arrangements, nothing was done afterwards. After this, father's behaviour (attitude) has changed. Says that he (father) has grown old and I am a liability for him."

Female younger generation respondent reported—

Illustration 7: "Everybody lives separately. Only when they start jointly to doing something/working then only they would come to know the difference. We are not able to contribute any income to the household. So, house hold expenditure could not be managed, separated due to abuse and conflicts."

In another case younger generation Female reported that—

Illustration 8: "There are some differences in our way of thinking. I have a daughter, and my husband is a driver earning Rs. 2000. I also work and earn Rs. 800 per month as domestic servant (dusting, cleaning) and save a sum of Rs. 500 per month now and deposits the same on the name

> of daughter. When it was a joint family nothing could be saved from the income. Mother-in-law and brother-in-law are dependents and, whatever father-in-law managed to save was spent on liquor. I had to manage the work at home also after returning back from the work. These people, father-in-law, brother-in-law, mother-in-law keep sitting idle and they feel annoyed whenever I say something to them. Exchange of verbal abuse has became a matter of daily routine. Tension was always there. So, we separated. Neither have they made an effort to communicate with us nor we."

The younger generation emphasizes individualism and perceives that the older generation emphasizes more on sub-unit collectivism and is religious also. Their subjective experience being that the older generation gives more preference to younger generation son, as a result of which there is tension, pain, negative behavioural consequences and they tend to avoid the situation.

Besides these differences there are some more differences in attitudes of the older generation and younger generations in terms of life styles, earning approach, work patterns and child rearing practices.

Work Pattern and Earning Approach: The older generation emphasizes on hard work, being engaged in some work throughout and never sits idle. For example, an older generation got education up to intermediate and worked as class three employees in railways and his son is a graduate and a private driver. He reports:

> ***Illustration 9:*** "I do not know what these people are up to? He had been working in the private sector, and worked there for two months and then left it. Cannot work at one workplace continuously. I am bearing the cost expenses of his family too, even at this age. He drink alcohol, uses bad and abusing language in the family. He is not bothered about maligning the family's reputation. When he had ran out of money/had no money left with him for gambling, once he tried to take away his wife's jewellery. Then his mother resisted and asked him not to do so, he hit her. Since then no one says a word to him, we used to avoid

him. It's like you do whatever you feel like doing, we have got nothing to do with it."

Another older generation reports:

> ***Illustration 10:*** "I believe in earning money through hard work, never sit idle and be engaged in something or the other. The son is interested in earning quick money by doing something big and when I try to convince/explain to him against it, a quarrel erupts and he asks me not to interfere in his matters.

However, results show that there seems to be no negative impact of the differences in the consensual process based on these differences.

Younger generation reports that—

> ***Illustration 11:*** "There are significant differences between my way of thinking and fathers. In the earlier times one could sustain a livelihood somehow by labour and hard work, without any investment of capital. Now-a-days, it is different, but he does not understand. He tells me work hard, hard work makes everything possible. Once, after much persuasion he gave me a sum of Rs. 2000 for investment. What is the value of Rs. 2000 now-a-days? I put up a fruit-stall and spent some amount on it, and rest was spent either gambling or on friends. My father daily either abuses or delivers sermons to me. Now, after this event I am not seeking assistance from my father either in cash or in kind. Still he is after me daily. One cannot even sit/reside peacefully at the house. He starts abusing even when I am watching T.V. or listening to music, after coming home from temple. Still he treats me as a child. At the different activities like gambling take place I also gamble. There is tension in intergenerational relations when (father) tries to reason out/or make me understand, or abuses. I also reciprocate the rough abuse and sometimes abuse takes place in physical form."

The older generations perceive that the younger generation is not showing respect which result in verbal abuse between generations, mutual trust between generations is at the lowest level which causes tensions in younger generations. Besides these differences, the decisions of one generation are perceived by the other as individualistic, while decision-makers persist it as collective oriented. So, both the generations define their relations in terms of not so good, O.K., normal and so-so.

Generally, on looking at the generic behaviour it is clear that the expectations of both generations are not fulfiled. Both the generation differ in their expectation related to functional process like economic, physical and emotional support, normative process (familial role and responsibility, obligations), attitude and values, life styles, earning approach, work patterns. Given these differences older generation perceives that younger generation giving priority to self, younger generation experiences exercise of power, and verbally abuse by older generation and coped up with situation by stopping the communication, some people report avoidance, and some through reactionary behaviour and experience conflict in Intergenerational relations.

Life Style and Saving: Generally, older generation prefers simple living and emphasis on savings but younger generation prefers status enhancement style of (hi-fi) life consumption etc. For example, *Illustration 12* (older generation):

> ***Illustration 12:*** "In reference to attitudes, the older generation puts greater priority on normal life and savings and perceive that the younger generation gives priority to status enhancement style of life, consumption oriented behaviour Tension is the outcome of such situations along with disrespect and distrust in intergenerational relations. They cope with such these situations through avoiding the situation and maintaining silence. Intergenerational relations will become normal after some time. But they subjectively experience unhappy feelings, and conflict."

In the Affectual process, based on these, dissatisfactory behaviour is perceived, the disrespect and differences in subjective experience of which is verbal abuse, crises situation and tension is the outcome. They define relations in terms of "not".

In this pattern of intergenerational relations, both the

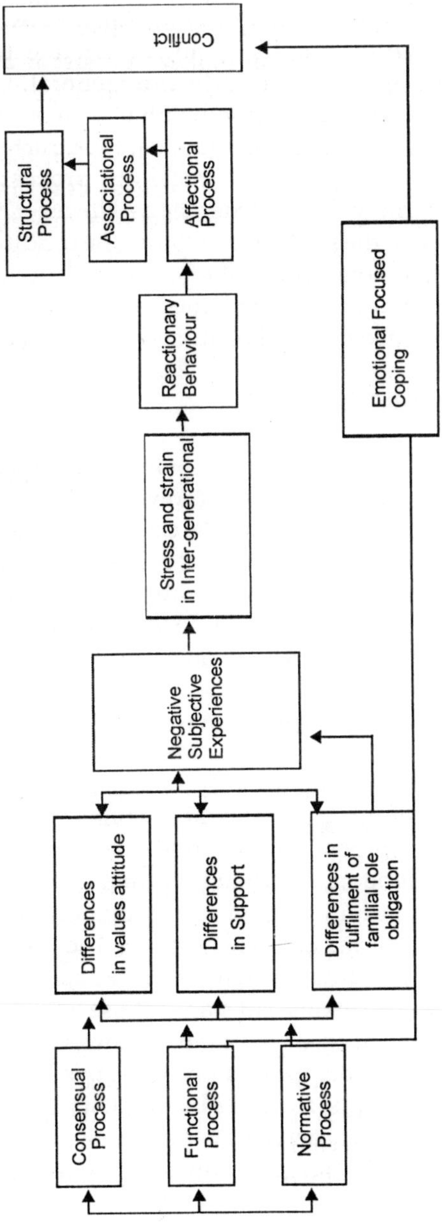

Fig. 6.1: Pictorial presentation of Process of Conflict in Intergenerational relationship

generations objectively have differences in terms of consensual process (values and attitudes), besides non-extension of support in terms of physical, emotional and economic (functional process), complementarity of role expectation and obligations between generations. Such a situation results in negative subjective experiences in relations and also stress in intergenerational relations. These stress and strains are coped with by reactionary mechanism that weakens the affectual, associational and structural processes at psychological level. Such wreaking process is manifested in terms of conflict between generations. However, the other possibility observed in the study is that under the condition of scarcity of resources and non-fulfilment of economic support, if coped through emotional focused coping mechanism then also the conflict pattern of intergenerational relations has emerged.

DISCUSSION

As per objective of the study to see the process of intergenerational conflict with demographic variations. Findings revealed that urban lower class family and some of the rural middle class families show the intergenerational conflict. Intergenerational conflict researches shows that conflict occurs when two generation people have different views, ideas or beliefs that are opposite to each other, people misunderstand each other and jump on wrong conclusions than conflict occurs.

Conflict experiencing family engages in ensured manual work in the unorganized sector and have manifested conflict pattern of intergenerational relations more significantly than the rural lower class family. This pattern of intergenerational relations is rooted in the non-fulfilment of reciprocity of obligations, i.e. though the older generation extends support, the younger generation fails to reciprocate it leading to non-fulfilment of reciprocal obligations in terms of physical, emotional and economic support. The younger generation besides their non-involvement in work, spend the money mostly on gambling, drinking, substance abuse but do not contribute to the substance need of the family. However, they expect contribution from the older generation. Thus, this leads to exchange of word, and to physical violence. This type of intergenerational relations was observed by Versa-Sanso (2007).

Figure 6.1 shows that both the generations objectively have

differences in terms of consensual process (values and attitudes), (normative process) non fulfilment of complementarity of role expectation and obligations between generations and on (functional process) not providing physical, emotional and economic support. Such a situation results in negative subjective experiences and stress and strain in intergenerational relations. These stress and strains, in response to these stressful situations, generation show reactionary mechanism or used emotional focused coping, weakens the affectual, associational and structural processes at psychological level. Such wreaking process is manifested in terms of conflict between generations. However, the other possibility observed in the study is that under the condition of scarcity of resources and non-fulfilment of economic support, if the situation is coped through emotional focused coping mechanism then also the conflict pattern of intergenerational relations will emerge.

So, in conflict situation, generations experience the differences in consensual process, normative process and functional process that leads to stress and strain in relationship and the situation is coped with reactionary behaviour that leads to negative consequences in the affection association and structure solidarity and they experience conflict type of relationship (Stenmen, 1979; Chafetz, 1981; Collins, 1975; Dowd, 1980).

This conflict pattern of intergenerational relations can be explained through the social exchange theory (Homans, 1958; Thibaut & Killeey, 1959), dependency theory and need theory (Duetsch, 1975). All the three theories have certain common elements in terms of fulfilment of needs of both the partners in social interaction as long as profitable for both the generations or as long as dependency relation is working without crisis (Stenman,1979). Whenever, there is a crisis in terms of financial matter, illness or death of a person in a family or the interaction was costlier in the family or non-fulfilment of needs of one generation, it leads to conflict. In this study, also, it was found that there is a difference in the priority of values between generation on the consensual process and not extending physical, emotional and economic support to the older generation and non-fulfilment of complementarity of role expectation, both objectively and subjectively promote stress and strain in intergenerational relations, but not conflict directly as propounded by the above mentioned theories. The coping mechanisms are leading to manifested conflict between generations.

Conclusion

The study was intended to assess the process of intergenerational conflict in the social context with the demographic variations. The findings reveal that the urban lower class family and some of rural middle class families show the pattern of intergenerational conflict. The conflict experiencing group face the scarcity of resources, due to this generations feel insecure and have differences in consensual process, normative process and functional process which means individuals develop the tendency of individualism, withdraw from fulfilment of familial role responsibility and obligations and are not interested to support next generations which leads stress and strain in relationship. In response to stress and strain generation shows reactionary (verbal and physical abuse) behaviour and experience conflict in relationship.

7
Intergenerational Relations and Well-being

This chapter tries to comprehend the relationship between pattern of intergenerational relations and the role of demographic (Age, Socio-Economic Class, Gender, Location: Rural/Urban) variables on experience of well-being.

In the study of intergenerational relations and well-being, literature suggests that support which the children extend to their aged parents promotes better well-being. Besides this, research on reciprocity and social support in intergenerational relations existing in old age showed mixed pattern of findings. Some studies show that social support improves the psychological well-being of older people or buffers the impact of stressful events and increase self-esteem (Russell & Cautrona, 1991; Silverstein & Bengtson, 1994; Thompson & Holmes, 1996; Lowestein *et al.*, 2007). In contrast some of the findings suggest that social support has little influence on well-being (Dean *et al.*,1990; Krause *et al.*, 1990), and frequent interaction of elderly with their children does not increase the morale and well-being of elderly (Lee & Kuntz, 1978; Wood & Robertson, 1978). However, other findings showed that support received from their children for the satisfaction of basic needs increases loss of autonomy and stress among older people (Arling, 1987; Dunham, 1985; Green & Feld, 1989; Lee, Netzer & Coward, 1995). Social support from their adult children or over involvement of relatives might be a cause of distress in old person. Social support includes excessive dependency of elderly on their children and subverts their self-efficacy, undermines autonomy, self-esteem and increases feeling of guilt, incompetence resentfulness, loss of autonomy etc. (Krause, 1987; Treas & Bengtson, 1987; Vinokur & Vinkour, 1990). Whereas, Venkatraman (1995) found that emotional support from a spouse is more important in determining well-being of elderly than is support from one's children.

Intergenerational relations between old aged parents and their adolescent children are less cohesive and more complicating in nature as the adolescent children establish their own identity and value system through their interaction with peers and members outside the family for support, thereby, asserting their autonomy and independence from their parents. These conflicts reduce psychological well-being of old aged parents in the family (Collins & Russell, 1991; Fuligni, 1998; Greenberg & Chen, 1996). However, the caregiving studies show that, increased the additional responsibility to provide care to the grandchildren and their parents leads to increased economic load for even the basic necessities of the additional family members which can also be aggravated by additional economic costs for medical treatment, legal expenses for custody issues and the costs of physical and mental health problems of their grandchildren (Waldrop and Weber, 2001). Moreover, grandmother who retain the custody of their grandchildren often report symptoms of psychological distress and depression when compared to non-resident and co-residing grandmothers (Kelly, Whitley, Spie & Yorker, 2000; Waldrop & Weber, 2001).

Singh & Chaddha (2004) conducted a study to understand the intergenerational relationship from the perspective of life satisfaction, attitude and role expectation of the grandchildren towards their grandparents and *vice versa*. No difference was found in terms of role expectation, hope and health interaction between generations strengthening better understanding over a period of time. Whereas Ruiz & Silverstein (2007) report that children who reside with grandparents perceive greater family cohesion and decreased depressive symptoms. This pattern was particularly significant among children of single parent families found that greater cohesion with grandparents decreased the depressive symptoms particularly among grandchildren residing in single parent family. However, these positive effects of stronger ties with grandparents are particularly pronounced among children who have strong bonds with their parents.

Research from developing world reveals a picture of change and continuity in intergenerational relations. It indicated the persistence of family ties and support showing that majority of older people are living with their young and maintaining closer relations with their families. They also draw primary support from their family. On the other hand, studies revealed that the family support to the older generation is decreasing and is inadequate in many countries, thereby exposing older generation to vulnerable situations in day-to-day life events (Mason, 1991; Versa-Sanso, 2007).

In Indian joint family system, two or three generations live together, having their roles and responsibilities. For example in a family, father is generally perceived as bread winner while mother is responsible for the upbringing of the children, taking care of their needs, providing love, care and protection. Grandfathers play the role of the custodian of the culture and conventions (take care of the grandchildren in the absence of their parent, and socializing them) of the family and children in the family are expected to respect their elders and care for the younger ones and extend help at home whenever necessary and relations are hierarchal (Pandey, 2007). Review on intergenerational relations and well-being shows that the major variables which are used as indicator of well-being or define as well-being are social support, self-esteem, autonomy, life satisfaction and health. However, there are other variables also that are part of well-being, i.e. happiness, self-efficacy, life orientation and social relations. Family interaction process is guided by other social/demographic factors like (Age, Socio-Economic Class, Gender, and Location: Rural/Urban). So, the objectives of the study are:

- To see the impact of Intergenerational Relations on well-being.
- To see the role of Socio-Economic Status on experience of well-being.
- To see the role of Location (rural/urban) on experience of well-being.
- To see the role of gender (male/female) on experience of well-being
- To see the role of age (older/younger) on experience of well-being.

Method: As discussed in chapter two.

RESULT

In this section, two main issues have been discussed. First, the effect of pattern of intergenerational relations on the well-being of respondents and secondly, the interaction of socio-economic status, age, gender and residence of respondent with pattern of intergenerational relations and its interaction effect on the well-being. Two way interactions of the socio-economic status, age, gender and place of residence are also discussed.

Table 7.1: Differences in Different Patterns of Relationship on Well-being related Variables

Variables	*Pattern of Intergenerational Relationship*			
	Solidarity	*Ambivalence*	*Conflict*	*F*
Self-Esteem	21.21	19.12	15.17	35.96***
Social Relation	18.26	16.67	13.68	25.48***
Social Support	16.37	13.55	9.15	57.64***
Autonomy	20.61	20.40	19.00	2.72
Purpose of life	17.56	17.02	13.40	26.98***
Satisfaction with life	41.73	37.77	30.73	39.79***
Happiness	16.24	14.98	11.23	41.02***
Psychological Health	20.56	20.50	33.41	36.91***
Physical Health	16.74	19.67	27.63	35.42***
Total Score of well-being	**187.78**	**182.30**	**170.75**	**14.75*** **

***p<.001,**p<.01, *p<.05

Source: Developed by authors using data from the respondents.

Table 7.1 shows mean scores of solidarity, ambivalence and conflict type of inter-generational relations and the F ratio calculated for each dimension of the well-being. The F ratio revealed significant differences for all the variables of well-being (Self-esteem, Social Relations, Social Support, Purpose of Life, Satisfaction with Life, Happiness, Psychological and Physical Health). But on the dimension of autonomy, all the three groups showed much similarity. However, in the case of purpose of life, solidarity and ambivalence pattern of intergenerational relations have no significant difference, but differ significantly with experience of conflict pattern of intergenerational relationship. On overall well-being scores, solidarity and ambivalence group do not differ significantly, but they significantly differ in conflict experiencing group.

Table 7.2: Differences due to Socio-Economic Status on Well-being related Variables

Variables	*Socio- Economic Status*			
	Upper	*Middle*	*Low*	*F*
Self-Esteem	21.57	18.93	16.73	21.86***
Social Relation	18.59	16.60	14.75	17.77***
Social Support	16.56	13.28	11.31	25.75***
Autonomy	20.99	20.23	19.26	3.12**
Purpose of Life	17.95	16.82	14.41	18.89***
Satisfaction with Life	42.82	37.82	32.83	32.93***
Happiness	16.54	14.95	12.42	26.36***
Psychological Health	20.32	24.87	30.54	22.04***
Physical Health	16.28	19.51	25.10	22.48***
Total Score of Well-being	**191.6**	**183.01**	**177.35**	**22.48*****

***p<.001, **p<.01, *p<.05

Source: Developed by authors using data from the respondents.

In Table 7.2, F ratio in three socio-economic categories and their relations with the dimensions of well-being reveal that all the respondents of three socio-economic statuses differ significantly on all the dimensions of well-being. Mean compressions revealed that the higher socio-economic status respondents reported higher level of well-being than the respondents of middle socio-economic statuses and lower socio-economic statuses. The respondent of higher socio-economic status and middle socio-economic status do not differ significantly on the dimension of autonomy and purpose of life, but differ with lower socio-economic status respondents. On the total score of well-being, all the three groups differ significantly.

On the basis of F ratios in Table 7.3, it can be concluded that the younger generation experience better self-esteem, social relations, purpose of life, physical and psychological health than the older generations. However, there is no significant difference between generations on the well-being dimensions of social support, autonomy, satisfaction with life and happiness and total score of well-being.

Differences in (Rural and Urban) Well-being related Variables

Table 7.4 dealt with the main effects of location (Rural and Urban) of respondents on various dimensions of well-being. In the

Table 7.4, the F ratio revealed that the urban and rural respondents differed significantly on the self-esteem, psychological and physical health. The rural respondents experienced better self-esteem, physical and psychological health than the urban respondents. On other dimensions of well-being, total score of well-being shows that the rural and urban people have same trend in experience of well-being.

Table 7.3: Differences in Age (Older & Younger) on Well-being related Variables

Variables	*Age*		
	Old	*Young*	*F*
Self-Esteem	17.69	20.34	17.59***
Social Relation	15.77	17.43	8.79**
Social Support	13.06	14.24	3.08
Autonomy	19.86	20.42	.93
Purpose of Life	15.38	17.32	14.50***
Satisfaction with Life	37.15	38.24	.87
Happiness	14.47	14.70	.19
Psychological Health	27.75	22.99	12.38***
Physical Health	22.97	17.82	20.06***
Total Score of well-being	**184.1**	**183.5**	**.58**

***p<.001, **p<.01, *p<.05.

Source: Developed by authors using data from the respondents.

Table 7.4: Means and ANOVAs of the Main Effects of Location

Variable	*Location*		
	Urban	*Rural*	*F*
Self-Esteem	18.29	19.77	5.14*
Social Relation	16.39	16.81	.529
Social Support	13.32	13.98	.938
Autonomy	20.27	20.01	.214
Purpose of Life	16.16	16.54	.528
Satisfaction with Life	37.37	38.03	.318
Happiness	14.47	14.70	.179
Psychological Health	26.94	23.74	5.39*
Physical Health	21.58	19.18	4.00*
Total Score of well-being	**184.79**	**182.76**	**0.16**

***p<.001, **p<.01, *p<.05

Source: Developed by authors using data from the respondents.

Figure 7.1 shows that women experience lower levels of self-esteem than the men in families who are experiencing solidarity and conflict pattern of intergenerational relations. But men and women do not differ significantly on self-esteem when ambivalent pattern of intergenerational relations are found.

Figure 7.2 shows that in general, women have a lower self-

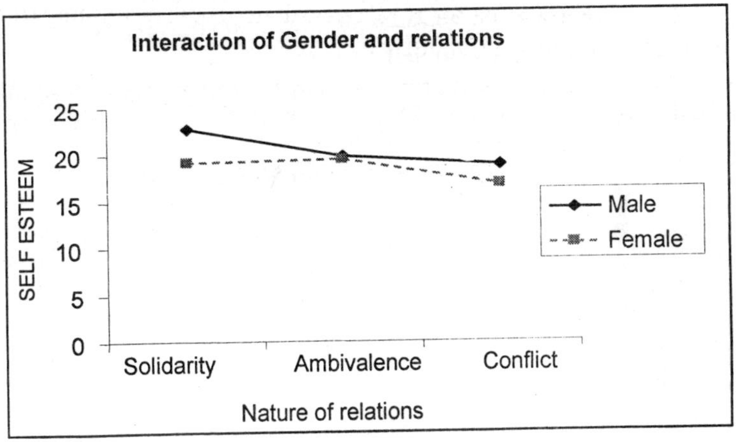

Fig. 7.1: Two Way Interaction Effects of Pattern of Intergenerational Relation and Gender

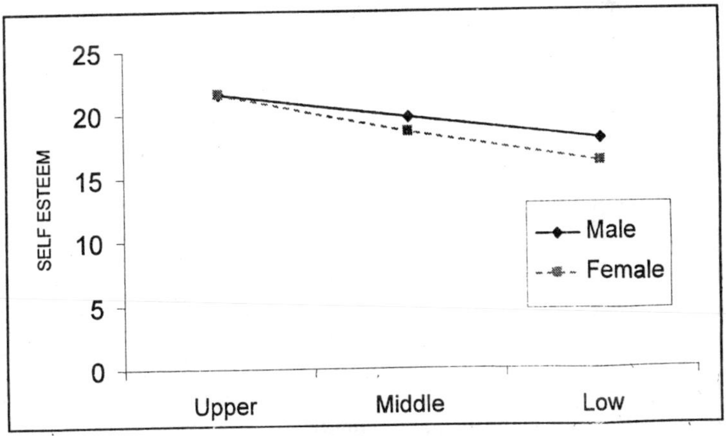

Fig. 7.2: Two Way Interaction Effects of Gender and Socio-economic Status

esteem than the men, but they differ on the basis of their socio-economic status. Both women and men in upper socio-economic status families have more or less same intensity of self-esteem. A declining trend in self-esteem is observed in the case of both women and men as observed between upper, middle and lower socio economic status. However, the intensity of decline in self-esteem is more intensive among women then the men.

Figures 7.3, 7.4, 7.5: Three-way Interaction of Age, Gender and Socio-economic Status on Self-Esteem

Figure 7.3 shows that older men of upper socio-economic status tend to have better self-esteem than the younger men, and

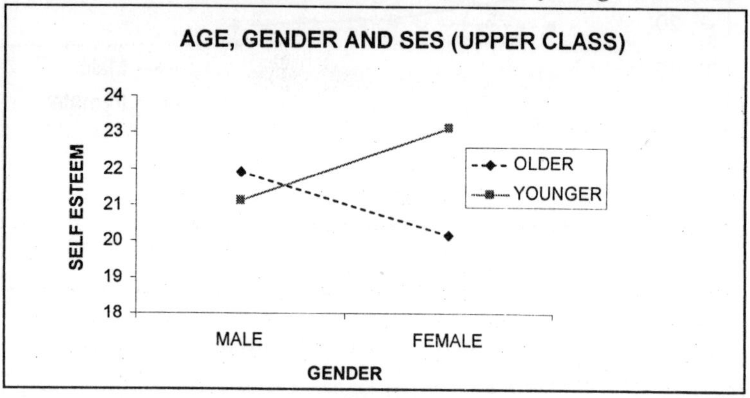

Fig. 7.3: Showing interaction among Age, Gender and Socio-economic status (Upper Class)

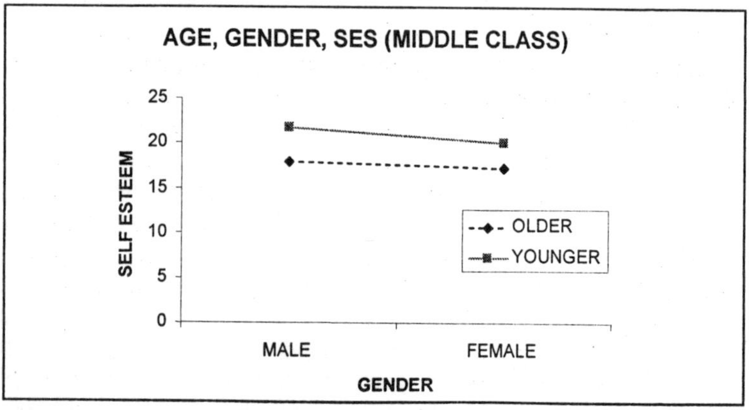

Fig. 7.4: Showing Interaction among Age, Gender and Socio-Economic status (Middle class)

younger women tend to have better self-esteem than the older women.

Figure 7.4 showed that in middle socio-economic status families, younger men and women both are experiencing better self-esteem than the older men and women. Younger men showed better self-esteem in comparison to younger women. Figure 7.5 showed that in lower socio-economic status families, younger men and women are experiencing higher self-esteem than the older men and women. But younger women enjoyed better self-esteem than the younger men. Older men experienced better self-esteem than the older women.

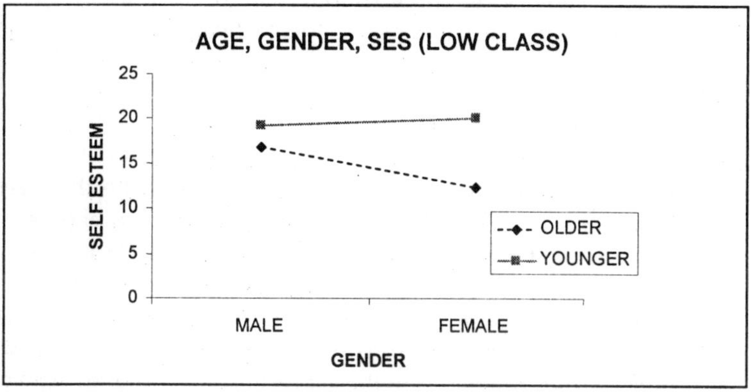

Fig. 7.5: Showing interaction between Age, Gender and Socio-Economic Status (Lower Class)

Mean score of male and female did not differ significantly for any aspects of the well-being.

In terms of interaction effect only self-esteem variable of well-being shows the significant difference.

DISCUSSION

Objective of the study was to see the impact of pattern of intergenerational relations (solidarity, conflict and ambivalence) on well-being, and study also tried to see the impact of demographic variables (age, gender, socio-economic status and location) on well-being.

Main findings of the study reveals that—

- Solidarity experiencing group had better well-being than ambivalence and conflict experiencing groups.
- Upper class families experienced better well-being than the middle and lower class families.
- In general older and younger generations experienced similar trend of well-being. However, younger generation experienced better well-being than the older ones on certain dimensions.
- Both rural and urban families have experienced similar trends of well-being. However rural families had better experiences on three dimensions of well-being (self-esteem, physical and psychological health) than the urban families.

Intergenerational Relations and Well-being

The result (1) showed the significant difference among the three groups (solidarity, ambivalence and conflict) based on pattern of intergenerational relations on overall well-being and also on various dimensions of well-being like self-esteem, social relations, social support, purpose of life, satisfaction with life, happiness, physical and psychological health. However, there is not any significant difference between these groups on the dimensions of autonomy. Autonomy is a dimension which has no impact of relationship pattern. A micro-analysis of three patterns of intergenerational relations revealed that all three groups experience similar kind of autonomy due to different reasons. Solidarity experiencing groups perceive autonomy due to no interference from family members and freedom to act and made decision independently while the conflict group act independently and make decisions freely due to their individualistic values.

The results clearly showed that those experiencing solidarity also showed highest level of well-being followed by those who experience ambivalence or conflict. The solidarity experiencing groups have shown better social relations and social support than other two groups, ambivalence and conflict, respectively. The solidarity group is better on normative, functional and consensual process which results in high level of understanding, trust, satisfaction closeness, cooperation and respect in relationship. This in turn resulted in better social relation and social support. Studies on intergenerational relations have found that if older generation experience support and social relations or care by younger generation, their well-being increases (Chaddha & Kolt, 2004; Lowenstein *et al.*, 2007).

Ambivalence group have differences on attitudes and values and lack in normative process (fulfilment of obligations, role and responsibility) so they experience less understanding, reciprocity, distance and other affects. Experiences showed that they experience less social support and social relations. The conflict group is mainly characterized by dissatisfaction in affectual process which results in less social support and social relations (Singh & Chaddha, 2004; Rikhye & Chaddha, 1998).

The solidarity group showed better self-esteem, social support, social relations, and satisfaction with life and happiness which resulted in better psychological health as compared to the other two groups. Other two groups (ambivalence and conflict) showed similar pattern as in other dimensions of well-being.

Better social and financial support experienced by solidarity group resulted in availability of medical facilities, nutritious food and better equipment to maintain their physical health. This kind of support were lower in ambivalence group and least in conflict experiencing group, which resulted in poor/worse physical health.

Socio-Economic Status and Well-being

The main three socio-economic status groups (upper, middle and lower) differed significantly on well-being and its various dimensions. But the upper socio-economic status and the middle socio-economic status group did not significantly differ on autonomy and purpose of life. But they differ significantly with the low socio-economic status group.

The respondents of upper socio-economic status group experienced better well-being and its various dimensions followed by middle and lower socio-economic status. The upper socio-economic group is able to fulfil their basic needs and have better control on familial life which results in positive self-image and self-esteem. According to Need-hierarchy theory higher needs can emerge only when the lower, basic needs have been adequately satisfied. When the basic needs and familial obligations are fulfilled, people perceive positive self-image, and better self-esteem (Maslow, 1970). Earlier studies in this area have reported that people with adverse socio-economic condition have negative self-image (Naidu, 1981; Dixit & Moorjani, 1981).

People from upper socio-economic level are highly satisfied with life and happier than the other two groups (middle and lower socio-economic status). This is because individuals with higher income level are better able to satisfy their needs and as a result are happy and better satisfied in their lives (Maslow, 1970; Veenhoven, 1995). Earlier researchers have also reported this trend where happiness levels tend to increase with increasing levels of income and prosperity (Veenhoven, 1991) whereas external or situational factors such as economic prosperity and income are generally viewed as a objective indicator of well-being and are known to have little impact on subjective well-being (Pavot & Diener, 1993; Diener & Diener, 1996). It means that income is positively related with happiness and satisfaction with life to a certain level, but after that level, other factors are also important. The present study found a linear relationship with socio-economic status. It may be due to social or economic structure in India. Income is as important as social support and social relations.

Table 7.2 indicates significant differences in level of socio-economic status on physical and psychological health. Upper socio-economic group have better employment, adequate medical care, nutrition, and better equipment's of shelter. So, they experience good physical health. Satisfaction with life, happiness, and other dimension of well-being are also high in upper social income group and this leads to high psychological health (Kitagwa & Hauser, 1973; Syme & Barkman, 1976).

Economic variable have close linkages with the dimensions of well-being. Upper socio-economic groups show high social relation and social support as compared to the low socio-economic group which showed lower social relation and social support. Supportive interaction and supportive relation in the family play a major role in well-being and health. The upper economic status enables people not only to fulfil their own needs but also help in fulfilling the needs and desire of their family members and through this mechanism, good social relations emerges. Upper socio-economic groups also provide enhanced support system, which alleviates distress and increases well-being (Sharma, 1999).

Table 7.2 reflects that higher socio-economic status and middle socio-economic status groups perceive the same kind of autonomy. Upper and middle socio-economic group had sufficient earnings to meet their needs and have control on their familial liabilities. So, both the group feels the same kind of autonomy. Low socio-economic group are unable to fulfil their needs and perceive familial obligations as a burden and so they perceive lesser autonomy. The socio-economic status also influences future orientation. Low socio-economic groups are earning meager amount of money which is not even sufficient to substantiate their daily needs. Mostly, earnings of low socio economic group are less than the subsistence requirements and results in lack of control on their family life. They want to get out from this situation but they have no hope for it. These conditions make them pessimistic towards future life. The other two groups, i.e. upper and middle socio economics group have sufficient amount of money not only to meet their daily expenses but also to plan their future. It makes them optimistic towards future life. So the purpose of life was found to be better in higher and middle socioeconomic status and poorer in lower socio-economic status (Sinha, 1969; Antonucci, *et al.*, 2003).

Age and Well-being

Table 7.3 showed that the means of older and younger generation show that both groups significantly differ on dimensions such as self-esteem, social relations, purpose of life, physical and psychological health, whereas, they did not differ significantly on such dimensions like, happiness, satisfaction with life, autonomy, social support and overall well-being. The internal means comparison showed that younger generation have better overall well-being and its dimensions as compared to older generation.

A review of relevant literature showed that there is complex relationship in age and subjective well-being. It has been found that individuals of younger age tend to be happier than those who are older (Bradburnand & Caplovitz, 1965). On the other hand, many other studies have not found evidence for any association between age and well-being (Alston *et al.* 1974; Andrews & Withey, 1976). However, several studies have also found positive association between age and satisfaction (Clements & Saur, 1976a;

Medly, 1980). Diener *et al.,* (2002) argue that relationship on age and well-being depends on component of subjective well-being measure. In this study, the younger are much better on self-esteem, social relation, purpose of life, psychological as well as physical health. It can be explained by the fact that they had strong feeling of control, independence and participate in various activities due to their physical fitness. Younger people have control in the family. They earn money. So, they have positive self-image, good physical and psychological health and better purpose of life. There was no significant difference on Satisfaction with life and happiness, autonomy and social support between two generations. Diener and Such (1998) have also found evidence for the fact that positive affect decreases with increasing age. However, they found that life satisfaction and unpleasant affect remains unchanged with increasing age.

Location and Well-being

The means of main effects of rural and urban background on well-being and its various dimensions are presented in Table 7.4. The means of both rural and urban showed that both groups do not differ significantly on dimensions like social support, social relations, autonomy, purpose of life, satisfaction with life and over all well-being, but the two groups differ significantly on dimensions like self-esteem, physical and psychological health. The rural people had higher means on these dimensions of well-being as compared to urban people. According to activity theory, rural people were engaged in agricultural work that requires more activities and these activities result probably in a better physical health. They were engaged, which gives them a sense of independence and they feel that they are not burden on anyone and can take care of themselves. This also resulted in their better self-esteem and better psychological health (Diener *et al.,* 2002). The other dimensions of well-being are not significantly different in location related groups. However, the rural people are better on the dimensions like social relation, social support, autonomy, purpose of life, happiness, satisfaction with life than the urban people as is evident from the means. One possible reason could be that urban people were mostly rural migrants so they perceive similar kind of life style and feel similar kind of well-being.

Another micro-level of analysis of the sample reveals that the literacy rate (urban male = 73.6% and female = 42.9%) and (rural male = 74.4% and female = 50.1%) and household size 7 are almost same in rural and urban areas. In rural setting there is less stressful situation so they feel better on various dimensions of well-being. Over all, well-being of rural and urban people does not differ significantly. This shows that urban and rural people have similar experience of well-being.

Gender (Male/Female) and Well-being

The results showed that there are no significant differences between male and female on the total score of well-being and its dimensions. One reason that can be speculated is that the family is a unit and both the gender interact in a similar way and they have similar experiences. Figure 7.1 also showed that both the gender show same pattern of intergenerational relations so they experience similar kind of well-being.

Two Way Interaction Effect of Pattern of Intergenerational Relation and Gender

Figure 7.1 showed that women experience lower levels of self-esteem than the men in families that are experiencing solidarity and conflict pattern of intergenerational relations. But, men and women did not differ significantly on self-esteem when ambivalent pattern of intergenerational relations are found. The main cause may be that society is male dominant and male members are earning members, having authority and power for decision-making and thus having higher self-esteem as compared to women. Another reason can be that solidarity group people have respect, authority, autonomy and positive experiences that lead to better self-esteem and just opposite in conflict experiencing group. Whereas, in ambivalence situation both male and female are dependent on next generation and experience loss of power and autonomy for male and female. So, they have equal experience of self-esteem.

Two way interactions of Gender and Socio-Economic Status

Figure 7.2 showed that in general women have a lower self-esteem than the men, but they differ on the basis of their socio economic status. Both women and men in upper socio-economic status families have more or less similar self-esteem. This trend of decline in self esteem across socio-economic levels was seen in men as well as women. However, the intensity of decline in self-esteem is more intensive among women than the men. Generally, in the higher class, both male and female were independent and enjoy autonomy, freedom and fulfil their basic desires. However, in the middle and lower class, they were not able to fulfil their desire and remain dependent on the younger generation, so they experience lower self-esteem. In middle and lower class, females depend on the male family member and did not evaluate themselves positively. Though lower class female work, they perceive themselves as negatively because they are unable to fulfil their basic needs even though working. So, they experience poor self-esteem.

Three Way Interactions of Age, Gender and Socio-Economic Status

Figure 7.3 shows that older men of upper socio-economic status experience better self-esteem than the younger men, and younger women experience better self-esteem than the older women. Because the younger female came in the family from outside after marriage and they enjoy their freedom and autonomy whereas older female experience problems due to life style, perceived autonomy and individualism of younger female and have negative experience and had lower level of self-esteem. Both younger generation and older member had economic independence and autonomy, but younger generation perceives responsibility as burden and thus experience poor self-esteem.

Figure 7.4 revealed that in middle socio-economic status families, younger men and women both were experiencing better self-esteem than the older men and women. Younger men showed better self-esteem in comparison to younger women because in middle class family older generation was dependent on younger generation. Younger generations were earning members and they have power and authority and thus experience positive and better self-esteem. Whereas, younger women are household women and their husbands are employed so they use the power and authority of her husband in family and experience positive and better self-esteem. The older women experienced dual dependency on her son and her husband also and thus experience lower level of self-esteem.

Figure 7.5 showed that in lower socio-economic status families, younger men and women are experiencing higher self-esteem than the older men and women. But younger women experience little bit better self-esteem than the younger men. Older men experience better self-esteem than the older women. One of the reasons may be that the younger women in lower class were earning members; they earn livelihood that promotes their self-esteem as compared to younger male and older male and female. Because older female were dependent on younger female and they are not physically active, they experience lower levels of self-esteem. Younger male were also earning but they do not earn enough to fulfil their basic need and desire, and thus experience lower level of self-esteem compared to female. Older male were basically dependent and face problems due to dependency, scarcity of resources and perceive negatively poor self-esteem.

Conclusion

The findings of the study reveal that experience of pattern of intergenerational relations, and economic class affect the well-being. However location, gender and age show the nearly similar pattern experience of well-being. It means those who experienced better support, (economic, social and emotional) fulfilment of familial norms (familial obligations, role and responsibility) and similarities in values and attitude between generations; and ability to fulfil basic needs and economic independence experienced better well-being. However, rural-urban, male-female and older younger people have similar experiences on well-being.

8
Concluding Remarks and Future Direction of Research

We began this work with the objective to study the patterns and psycho-social process of intergenerational relations with demographic variations. Much of the intergenerational research seems to investigate the pattern of intergenerational relations with structural change in society on macro-level.

Findings highlighted the new trend of intergenerational relations more vividly. The pattern of intergenerational relations varied with demographic variables. The present study shows that most of the sampled households have experienced solidarity (42.7%), followed by ambivalence (32.97%) and conflict (24.86%). Furthermore, findings also show that the patterns vary along with class status and location of the family. Most of the urban upper class and rural upper and lower class family have demonstrated solidarity pattern of intergenerational relations. Middle class families, both in rural and urban areas, have shown mostly ambivalent pattern of intergenerational relations. However, the urban lower class family has shown conflict pattern of intergenerational relations.

In context of solidarity, urban and rural upper class family have experienced interdependency as well as mutual fulfillment of familial obligations and extending functional support. Besides this, both generations respect the autonomy of each other. It has also been noted that emotional interdependence between generations is one of the major contributing factor in promoting interpersonal connectedness and solidarity. The joint families are in the process of becoming nuclear; however, they function through emotional bonding and materialistic interdependency, and maintain functional support (reciprocal fulfillment of familial obligations) which in turn leads to intergenerational and family solidarity.

However, the rural lower class family are also showing solidarity pattern of intergenerational relations. Most of the families are landless and are labourers. Their employment is seasonal and there is hardly any employment security. Consequently, some of the young male members migrate to other state such as Gujarat and Bengal in search of manual work. In general, the wife and children of migrant worker stays with in-laws and is taken care by the husband's family. Until the migrant worker gets full employment, his wife and children are looked after by his family. The migrant worker reciprocates this concern by sending remittance to the family. Thus, through the monetary contribution, they fulfil the reciprocity of filial obligations in meeting out the basic needs and enhancing the status of family in village community and caste.

Rural and urban middle class family have manifested ambivalence pattern of intergenerational relations. The ambivalence pattern of intergenerational relations is a consequence of subjective and objective level of fulfilment of reciprocity of family obligations, support and normative process. Though middle class families are satisfied with emotional dependency, but they are dissatisfied on the issues of material interdependency, discrepancy of values and attitude. Middle class families are experiencing both functional and emotional dependency, but dissatisfied with the extent of functional support extended to them by the younger generation. Also, the older generation would like to see their children autonomous and independent but at the same time prefer to retain authority. Such situations lead to ambivalent pattern of intergenerational relation.

Most of the urban lower class families engage in ensured manual work in the unorganized sector and have manifested conflict pattern of intergenerational relations more significantly than the rural lower class family. This pattern of intergenerational relations is rooted in the non-fulfillment of reciprocity of obligations, i.e. though the older generation extends support, the younger generation fails to reciprocate it leading to the non-fulfilment of reciprocal obligations in terms of physical, emotional and economic support. The younger generation besides their non-involvement in work, spend the money mostly on gambling, drinking, and substance abuse. They do not contribute to the substance need of the family. However, they expect contribution from the older generation. This leads to discordant relationship between younger and older generation and sometimes take the form of physical assault. In total, three important outcomes can be derived. First, interdependency, support, fulfillment of obligations, and reciprocity leads to solidarity. Second, the subjective perception of non-fulfilment of reciprocities obligations between generations leads to ambivalence. Third, one-sided fulfilment of obligations may result in conflict between generations.

In the process of different types of intergenerational relations, findings show that in the context of solidarity, generations have difference in values and attitude which leads to negative subjective experiences, and stress and strain in relationship. To minimize stressful experiences, generations used problem focused coping approach to maintain affection and association, which, in turn, leads to solidarity in relationship. Whereas in context of ambivalence generations have differences in values, attitude, perception of fulfillment of familial role, responsibility, and obligations, which negatively affects the subjective experiences and causes stress in relationship. To alleviate this stress, people used emotional focused coping, live with dissatisfaction, and have both love and hate feelings, which leads to ambivalence in relationship. However, in the context of conflict, the same stressful situation is combated through reactionary behaviour and exchange of hard voices which in turn effects the affection and association of generations that furthers the conflict in relationship. It means that in consensual level differences, generations used problem focused coping approach, in normative level differences, generations used emotional focused coping approach and in functional level differences, generations used reactionary behaviour. Besides this, if generations have differences in functional level over monetary issue and they use emotional focused coping, then also conflict type of intergenerational relationship is demonstrated.

With reference to intergenerational relations and well-being, findings reveal that different patterns of intergenerational relations experienced and economic class affects the well-being. However, location, gender, and age also affect well-being in a similar way. It means those who experienced better support (economic, social and emotional), fulfillment of familial norms (familial obligations, role and responsibility), similarities in values and attitude between generations, and ability to fulfil basic needs and economic independence experienced better well-being. However, all respondents be it rural-urban, male-female or old-young, had similar pattern of experiences on well-being.

Limitation and Further Research

The phenomenon of intergenerational relations has attracted attention due to rapid demographic transition of population in countries like India. Intergenerational relations are influenced by a combination of factors. This study attempts to understand some of the factors influencing pattern and processes of intergenerational relations, and its impact on well-being of generations. The multifaceted phenomenon of intergenerational relations cannot be understood in a single study. Therefore, this study has some of the following limitations:

- India is a land of festivals and rituals where celebration is a way of life. Ceremonies on the occasions of marriage and birth, and festivals manifest different shades of intergenerational relations within the family and kin group. Its inclusion in intergenerational issues may throw some important insights about the phenomena.
- Besides narrative method, other qualitative methods such as observations and conversation analysis may also reveal newer aspects of intergenerational relations.
- In order to expand the generalization and acceptability, further studies are suggested on a larger sample size, as well as the use of other qualitative methods such as grounded theory would be insightful.
- The socio-economic condition was considered a major influencing factor of intergenerational relations in this study. The role of caste and education in intergenerational relations could be another issue which needs further probing.

- The consumption pattern is defined in the present study on the basis of ownership of major consumer goods (A.C., Car, T.V., Refrigerator,). Measures of the consumption pattern through uniform recall period (URP) and Mixed recall period (MRP) may contribute in identifying socio-economic status of sample households.
- Further studies on intergenerational relations within cosmopolitan and metropolitan sample and their comparative analysis may provide a better view of intergenerational issues. Related to this is the examination of the role of cross-cultural framework on intergenerational relations may provide a cultural standpoint.

Annexure 1

NARRATIVE INTERVIEW SCHEDULE

Narratives were taken from respondents, related to the following points:

- Description about family members, about their behaviour and occupation.
- Differences and similarities the respondent perceived with his next generation, giving examples in terms of behaviours.
- Behavioural outcome of this relationship (tension or conflict or harmony) and how the respondent coped with these situations, with experienced examples.
- Decision-making in the family, conflicts during the process of decision-making, and how the respondents resolve this conflict (with experienced examples).

Some issues were probed which were especially related to women like:

- What are the differences and similarities in behavioural pattern related between the place of origin and the husband's house?
- Who looks after the children and prepares them for school?

Annexure 2

SOCIAL PSYCHOLOGICAL STUDY ON INTERGENERATIONAL RELATIONS

Family is an organization and a community and this questionnaire is related to views regarding familial relations. In a family, member belonging to different age groups live together and interact with each other. In this interaction a person experiences few things in the context of intergeneration relationships. These experiences either have a positive impact on the person or negative. What impact does interaction occurring in your family has on your well-being.

In this context, some questions related to well-being are given below. How do you feel in context of these questions, please mark your responses by putting a ✓ mark on anyone of the options given in the scale right next to the question.

For example,

I feel that I have many good qualities in me.

(A) Very less, (B) less, (C) more, (D) much more

If you agree with the given statement mildly then put a √ on 1-very less, if you agree with the statement slightly then put a √ on 2-less. If you agree with the statement strongly then put a √ on 3-more, if you agree with statement very strongly then put a √ on 4-much more. There is no right or wrong answer; we only intend to get an insight into your thoughts.

THANK YOU

Sunil Kumar Verma
Research Scholar, Department of Psychology
Allahabad University, Allahabad

Demographic Details

Before beginning the questionnaire, please fill in the following details:

Personal Details	*Age....*	***Condition of the House***	
Gender	Male.... Female....	1. Clay/ Brick/ Tile/ Hut	
	Urban.... Rural....	2. Self owned/ Rented	
Religion	Hindu.... Muslim.... Christian.... Sikh....	3. Number of rooms	
Cast....................		4. When was it constructed	
Type of Family	Nuclear.... Joint..... Extended Joint.....	5. It is located in which area of the city.	

Family Details

Serial No.	*Name of the Family Members*	*Gender*	*Relationship with the Respondent*	*Educational Qualifications*	*Job*	*Annual Income*

Economic Conditions (What all things you have in your house)

Items	*Number of items*	*What is the brand?*	*New or Old*	*When was it purchased?*	*Who bought it?*
A.C.					
Car/Tractor					
T.V.					
Music system/ radio					
Scooter/ Motorcycle					
Fridge					

Washing Machine					
Inverter/ Generator					
Telephone					
Gas					
Tube-well Boring					
Thresher					
Diesel Engine/ Pump-set					
Cycle					
Farmland area					
Bullock cart					
Dairy Cattle					
Farm Animals					
Computer					

1. I consider myself better than the people around me
   1. Very less 2. Less 3. More 4. Much more
2. I think it's painful to maintain close relationships.
   1. Very less 2. Less 3. More 4. Much more
3. I feel that I have a number of good qualities.
   1. Very less 2. Less 3. More 4. Much more
4. I feel I have very few close people I can share my worries with.
   1. Very less 2. Less 3. More 4. Much more
5. I have knowledge of my life and its direction.
   1. Very less 2. Less 3. More 4. Much more
6. I often feel lonely within my family.
   1. Very less 2. Less 3. More 4. Much more
7. I feel I do not have much to be proud of.
   1. Very less 2. Less 3. More 4. Much more
8. I do not have any knowledge about what I want to achieve in my life.
   1. Very less 2. Less 3. More 4. Much more
9. I make sure to listen carefully when my friends are sharing their highs and lows with each other.
   1. Very less 2. Less 3. More 4. Much more
10. I take a positive attitude towards myself.
    1. Very less 2. Less 3. More 4. Much more

11. I feel that I only have a few close people that I can trust.
    1. Very less 2. Less 3. More 4. Much more
12. I like to achieve my goals by making them in future context.
    1. Very less 2. Less 3. More 4. Much more
13. I feel that I am unable to implement my ideas because of my family's views and behaviour.
    1. Very less 2. Less 3. More 4. Much more
14. On the whole, I am satisfied with my self.
    1. Very less 2. Less 3. More 4. Much more
15. I think that I am not afraid to express my views even if they tend to differ from my family's views.
    1. Very less 2. Less 3. More 4. Much more
16. I feel it is a waste of time to make plans about things in the future context.
    1. Very less 2. Less 3. More 4. Much more
17. I feel that my family's views and decisions do not have any effect on me.
    1. Very less 2. Less 3. More 4. Much more
18. I feel that all my decisions are dependent on my parents and family's happiness.
    1. Very less 2. Less 3. More 4. Much more
19. I am quite active in bringing the plans laid down by me to completion.
    1. Very less 2. Less 3. More 4. Much more
20. I certainly feel useless at time.
    1. Very less 2. Less 3. More 4. Much more
21. I feel that I have complete confidence in my own ideas and decisions even if they are opposite from my family's ideas.
    1. Very less 2. Less 3. More 4. Much more
22. I feel disappointed that I could not do anything in my life.
    1. Very less 2. Less 3. More 4. Much more
23. I feel that my relatives trust each other.
    1. Very less 2. Less 3. More 4. Much more
24. All in all I feel that I am an unsuccessful person.
    1. Very less 2. Less 3. More 4. Much more

25. I feel that I get the support that I expect from my family.
    1. Very less 2. Less 3. More 4. Much more
26. I feel that I am happy fulfilling my familial responsibilities.
    1. Very less 2. Less 3. More 4. Much more
27. I would not want any changes in my past.
    1. Very less 2. Less 3. More 4. Much more
28. I feel that I am not happy with my familial relations.
    1. Very less 2. Less 3. More 4. Much more
29. I feel that at times of financial crisis my family members help me out.
    1. Very less 2. Less 3. More 4. Much more
30. I am satisfied with my past.
    1. Very less 2. Less 3. More 4. Much more
31. I feel that my family members are unable to make me do something that I do not want to do.
    1. Very less 2. Less 3. More 4. Much more
32. My past years have been ideal for me.
    1. Very less 2. Less 3. More 4. Much more
33. In the past, my life circumstances were the best.
    1. Very less 2. Less 3. More 4. Much more
34. In the past I had all those things (important things) that I desired.
    1. Very less 2. Less 3. More 4. Much more
35. I feel happy with my familial achievements.
    1. Very less 2. Less 3. More 4. Much more
36. I feel that whenever I am mentally distressed, my family members support me.
    1. Very less 2. Less 3. More 4. Much more
37. At present I do not want to change anything in my life.
    1. Very less 2. Less 3. More 4. Much more
38. Presently I am satisfied with my life.
    1. Very less 2. Less 3. More 4. Much more
39. My life, at present, is ideal for me.
    1. Very less 2. Less 3. More 4. Much more
40. I feel loved by my family members whenever I need it.
    1. Very less 2. Less 3. More 4. Much more

41. At present, I am at my best in my life.
    1. Very less 2. Less 3. More 4. Much more
42. At present, I have everything (important things) that I desire.
    1. Very less 2. Less 3. More 4. Much more
43. I feel that I do not change my way of thinking due to familial pressure.
    1. Very less 2. Less 3. More 4. Much more
44. There is nothing I would like to alter in the future.
    1. Very less 2. Less 3. More 4. Much more
45. I feel that I do not change my way of working due to familial pressure.
    1. Very less 2. Less 3. More 4. Much more
46. In the future, I will be satisfied with my life.
    1. Very less 2. Less 3. More 4. Much more
47. I hope my future will be ideal for me.
    1. Very less 2. Less 3. More 4. Much more
48. In the future, my life circumstances will be the best for me.
    1. Very less 2. Less 3. More 4. Much more
49. In the future, I will be having all those things (important things) that I desire.
    1. Very less 2. Less 3. More 4. Much more
50. I think that I'm happy with my married life.
    1. Very less 2. Less 3. More 4. Much more
51. I feel that whenever I need it, my family members love and support me.
    1. Very less 2. Less 3. More 4. Much more
52. I am happy with my socio-economic conditions.
    1. Very less 2. Less 3. More 4. Much more

Reaction Measurement Scale

Instructions: Given below are statements related to your feelings. Please reply keeping in minds your feelings over the past one-month.

53. Feel nervous.
    1. Very less 2. Less 3. More 4. Much more
54. Do not feel happy.
    1. Very less 2. Less 3. More 4. Much more
55. Not able to sleep properly.
    1. Very less 2. Less 3. More 4. Much more
56. Get angry easily.
    1. Very less 2. Less 3. More 4. Much more
57. Feel tensed without reason.
    1. Very less 2. Less 3. More 4. Much more
58. Cannot concentrate in whatever work I do.
    1. Very less 2. Less 3. More 4. Much more
59. Feel tensed.
    1. Very less 2. Less 3. More 4. Much more
60. Get irritated easily.
    1. Very less 2. Less 3. More 4. Much more
61. Feel depressed.
    1. Very less 2. Less 3. More 4. Much more
62. Tend to feel uneasy.
    1. Very less 2. Less 3. More 4. Much more
63. Feel suffocated.
    1. Very less 2. Less 3. More 4. Much more

Physical Symptoms

Instructions: Given below are a few statements related to physical problems. Please tell us over the past one month how often you experienced these problems.

64. Tend to experience body ache.
    1. Very less 2. Less 3. More 4. Much more
65. Tend to feel dizzy.
    1. Very less 2. Less 3. More 4. Much more
66. Get fatigued soon.
    1. Very less 2. Less 3. More 4. Much more
67. Experience chest pain.
    1. Very less 2. Less 3. More 4. Much more

68. Experience heavy breathing.
    1. Very less 2. Less 3. More 4. Much more
69. Tend to have upset stomach.
    1. Very less 2. Less 3. More 4. Much more
70. Tend to fall ill soon.
    1. Very less 2. Less 3. More 4. Much more
71. Do not to feel hungry properly.
    1. Very less 2. Less 3. More 4. Much more
72. Experience headache.
    1. Very less 2. Less 3. More 4. Much more
73. Tendency towards boil formation.
    1. Very less 2. Less 3. More 4. Much more

Description of Scale

Variables	*No. of Items*	*Items No.*
Self-esteem	7	1, 3, 7*, 10, 14, 20*, 24*
Social relation	6	2*, 4*, 6*, 9, 11*, 23
Social support	5	25, 29, 36, 40, 51,
Autonomy	8	13*, 15, 17, 18, 21, 31, 43, 45
Purpose of life	6	5, 8*, 12, 16*, 19, 22*
Happiness	5	26, 28*, 35, 50, 52
Satisfaction with life	15	Past: (27, 30, 32, 33, 34)
		Present: (37, 38, 39, 41, 42)
		Future: (44, 46, 47, 48, 49)
Health Psychological	11	53, 54, 55, 56, 57, 58, 59, 60, 61, 62, 63
Physical	10	64, 65, 66, 67, 68, 69, 70, 71, 72, 73.

Note: * Items are reversely coded.

Bibliography

Abraido-Lanza, A.F., Guier, C. & Revenson, T.A. (1996). Coping and social support resources among Latins with arthritis, *Care and Research*, 9, 501-508.

Ajrouch, K.J. (2007). Health disparities and Arab-American elders: Does intergenerational support buffer the inequality-health link? *Journal of Social Issues*, 63, 745-748.

Aldous, J. & Hill, R. (1965). Social cohesion, lineage type, and intergenerational transmission. *Social Forces, 43,* 471-482.

Aldwin, C. & Greenberger, E. (1987). Cultural differences in the predictors of depression. *American Journal of Community Psychology,* 37, 789-813.

Alston, J. P., Lowe, G. D. & Wrigly, A. (1974). Socio-economic Correlates For four Dimensions of Self-Perceived Satisfaction, 1972. *Human Organization*, 33, 99-102.

Altbach, P. & Peterson, P. (1972). Before Berkeley: Historical perspective on American student activism. In P. Altbach & R. Laufer (Eds.), *The New Pilgrims: Youth Protest in Transition.* New York: David McKay.

Ananthraman, R.N. (1978). Perception of old age by two generations. *Journal of Psychological Research*, 23 (3), 31-38.

Andrews, F.M. &Withey, S.B. (1976) *Social Indicators of well-being: America's Perception of Life Quality*, New York: Plenum Press.

Angel, J., & Angel, R.J. (1992). Age at immigration, social connections, and well-being among elderly Hispanics. *Journal of Aging and Health*, 4, 480-499.

Ansello, E. (1980). Special considerations in rural aging, *Educational Gerontology*, 5(4), 343-354.

Antonucci, T. C., Kristine, J. A., & Janevic, M. R. (2003). The Effect of Social Relations with Children on the Education-Health Link in Men and Women Aged 40 and Over," *Social Science & Medicine*, 56, No. 5, 949-60.

Arling, G. (1987) Strain social support, and distress in old age. *Journal of Gerontology*, 42, 107-113.

Arnett, J.J. (1999). Adolescent storm and stress, reconsidered. *American Psychologist*, 54, 317-326.

Austein, W. (1979). Justice, freedom and self-interest in intergroup conflict. In W.G. Austein & S. Worchel (Eds.) *The Social Psychology of Intergroup Relations* (pp. 121-143), Monterey CA: Brooks/Cole.

Bawin-Legros, B., & Stassen, J.F. (2002). Intergenerational solidarity between the family and the state. *Current Sociology*, 50, 243-262.

Beckman, L.J. (1981) Effect of social interaction and children's relative inputs on older women's psychological well-being. *Journal of Personality and Social Psychology*, 41, 1075-1086.

Bell, J. (Ed.) (1997). A city for all: Valuing differences and working with diversity. London: Zed Books.

Bengtson, V. L. (1973). *The Social Psychology of Aging*. Indiana Polis: Bobbs-Merrill.

Bengtson, V.L. (1975). "Generation and Family Effects an Value Socialization." *American Sociological Review*, 40: 358-71.

Bengtson, V. & Black, K.D. (1973). Intergenerational relations and continuities in socialization. In W. Schaie & P. Baltes (Eds.), *Personality and Socialization*. New York: Academic Press.

Bengtson, V.L. & Cutler, N. (1976). Generations and intergenerational relations: Perspective on age group and social change. In R. Binstock & E. Shanas, (Eds.), *Handbook of Aging and the Social Science* (pp. 130-159). New York: Van Nostrand Reinhold.

Bengtson, V.L., Furlong, M.J., & Laufer, R.S. (1974). Time, aging, and continuity of social structure: Theme and Issues in Generational Analysis. *Journal of Social Issues*, 30(2).

Bengtson, V. & Kuypers, J. (1971). Generational differences and the developmental state. *International Journal of Aging and Human Development, 2(4)*, 249-260.

Bengtson, V.L. & Kuypers, J.A. (1986). The family support cycle: Psycho-social issues in the aging family. In J.M.A. Munnichs, P. Mussen, & E. Olbrich (Eds.), *Life Span and Change in a Gerontological Perspective* (pp. 61-77). New York: Academic Press.

Bengtson, V.L. & Schroder, S. (1982). Parent-child relations: The measurement of intergenerational interaction and affect in old age. In D. Mangen & W. Peterson (Eds.), *Research Instruments in Social Gerontology*. Minneapolis: University of Minnesota Press.

Bengtson, V., Giarrusso, R., Marby, J. B. & Silverstein, M. (2002). Solidarity conflict and ambivalence: Complementary or competing perspective on intergenerational relations? *Journal of Marriage and Family, 64*, 568-576.

Berger, B. M. (1971). Hippie morality-more old than new. In Friedenberg (Ed.), *The Anti-American Generation*. New York: Transaction Books.

Berger, B.M. & Hackett, B.M. (1974). On the decline of age grading in rural Hippie communes. *Journal of Social Issues,* 30(2).

Bhingradiya, P. & Kamala, R. (1997). An intergenerational study on the situation of the elderly in rural Saurashtra. *Indian Journal of Gerontology,* 11 (3 & 4), 78-84.

Bleuler, E. (1911). *Dementia praecox oder groop schizphrenien* (Dementia praecox of the group of Schizophrenia). Leipzg Und Wien: Franz Deuticke.

Bradburn, N.M. & Caplovitz, D. (1965). *Reports on Happiness.* Chicago: Aldine.

Brannen, J. (2006). Cultures of Intergenerational transmission in four-generation families. *Sociological Review,* 134-154.

Brannen, J., Moss, P. & Mooney, A. (2004), Working and Caring Over the Twentieth Century: Change and Continuity in Four-Generation Families Palgrave.

Brannen, J. & Nilsen, A. (2002). Young People's Time Perspectives: From Youth to Adulthood, in *Sociology,* 36 (3), pp. 513-538.

Brewer, M. B., Dull, V., & Lui, L. (1981). Perceptions of the elderly: Stereotypes as prototypes. *Journal of Personality and Social Psychology,* 41, 656-670.

Brown, J. (1973). The value and norms of the expressive student sub-culture. *Youth and Society, 4,* 483-498.

Bryman, A. (1988a). *Quantity and Quality in Social Research.* London: Unwin Hyman.

Butler, R.N. (1969). Age-ism: Another form of bigotry: *Gerontologist,* 9, 243-46.

Carver, C.S., & Scheier, M.F. (1994). Situational coping and coping disposition in a stress transaction. *Journal of Personality and Social Psychology,* 66, 184-195.

Chaddha, N.K. & Mongia, R. (1997). Intergenerational solidarity. *Indian Journal of Medical Research,* 106, 370-375.

Chaddha, N.K. & Kolt, G.S. (2004). Intergenerational relationship building through physical activity. *Indian Journal of Gerontology,* 18: 3 & 4.

Chaddha, N.K. & Malik, N. (2004). Intergenerational relations: A futuristic framework, *Indian Journal of Gerontology, 18, 3&4,* 318-347.

Chafetz, J.S. (1981). Family conflict: The application of selected theories of social conflict to the understanding of conflicts in families. *Youth and Society, 13,* 157-171.

Chang, E.C. (1996). Cultural differences in optimism, pessimism and coping: Predictors of subsequent adjustment in Asian-American and Caucasian American students. *Journal of Counselling Psychology,* 43, 113-123.

Chang, E.C. (2001). A look at the coping strategies and style of Asian American: Similar and Different? In C.R. Cnyder (Eds.) *Coping with Stress: Effective People and Processes.* New York: Oxford University Press.

Chao, R.K. (2000). The parenting of immigrant Chinese and European American mothers: Relations between parenting style, socialization goals and parental practices. *Journal of Applied Developmental Psychology*, 21, 233-248.

Chappell, N.L. (1991). Role of family and friends in quality of life. In J.E. Birren & J.E. Lubben (Eds.) *Concept and Measurement of Quality of Life in Frail Elderly* (pp.171-190) San Diego, CA: Academic Press.

Chatman, S. (1978). *Story and Discourse: Narrative Structure in Fiction and Film*. Cornell: Cornell University Press.

Clements, F. & Sauer, W.J. (1976a). Life satisfaction in the United States. *Social Forces*, 54, 621-623.

Cohen, S. & Ganas, B. (1978). *The Other Generation Gap*. Chicago: Follett.

Cohler, B. (1983). Autonomy and interdependence in the family of adulthood. *The Gerontologist*, 23, 33-39.

Cohler, B.J. & Altergott, A.J. (1995). The family of second half of life: Connecting theories and findings. In R. Blieszner and V. Bedford (Eds.) *Handbook of Aging and Family* (pp. 59-94). Westport, CT: Greenwood Press.

Cohler, B.J. & Geyer, S. (1982). Psychological autonomy and interdependence within the family. In F. Wals (Ed.), *Normal Family Process* (pp. 196-226). New York: Gilford Press.

Cohort Study (1970). Conducted by National Child Development in Britain (p. 72.), cited in *Using Narrative in Social Research: Qualitative and Quantitative Approach* by Elliott, J. (2005), Sage.

Collins, R. (1975). *Conflict Sociology: Toward an Explanatory Science*. New York: Academic Press.

Collins, W.A. & Russell, G. (1991). Mother-child and father-child relationship in middle-hood and adolescence: A developmental analysis. *Developmental Review*, 11, 99-136.

Conger, R.D., Conger, K.J., Elder, G.H., Lorenz, J., Simmons, K.J. & Whiteback, R.L. (1993). Family economic stress and adjustment of early adolescent girls, *Developmental Psychology*, 29, 206-209.

Cooper, C.L., Dewe, P. & O'Driscoll, M. (2001). *Organizational stress: A Review and Critique of Theory, Research and Application*. California: Thousand Oaks.

Cottrell, L. (1942). The adjustment of the individual to his age and sex rates. *American Sociological Review, 7(5)*, 617-620.

Cowdry, E. (Ed.) (1939). *Problems of Aging*. Baltimore: William & Wilkins.

Cox, T., & Howarth, I. (1990). Organizational health, culture and helping. *Work and Stress*, 4(2), 107-110.

Coy, K. C., & Collins, W. A. (1998). Reconsidering changes in parent-child conflict across adolescence: A meta-analysis. *Child Development*, 69, 817–832.

Coyne, J.C., Wortman, C.B. & Lehman, D.R. (1988). The other side of support: emotional over-involvement and miscarried helping. In B.H.

Gottlieb (Ed.), *Marshalling Social Support: Formats, Processes and Effects* (pp. 305-331). Beverly Hills, CA: Sage.

Cross, S.E. (1995). Self-construal, coping and stress in cross-cultural adaptation. *Journal of Cross-Cultural Psychology*, 26, 673-679.

Cutrona, C.E. & Russel, D. (1990). Type of social support and specific stress: Toward a theory of optimal matching. In B.R. Saranson, I.G. Saranson and G.R. Pierce (Eds.) *Social Support: An International View* (pp. 319-366). New York: Wiely.

Cuyvers, P. (2000). You can't have it all- at least the some time. Segmentation in the modern life course as a threat of intergenerational communication and solidarity. In Tranka, S. (eds.) *Family Issue Between Gender & Generations*. Semina Report. Brussels: European Observatory on Family matters. European Commission, directorate—General for Employment and Social Affairs Unit E/1, pp. 30-43.

Daatland, S.O. & Herlofson, K. (2004). Familie, velferdsstat og aldring. Familiesolidaritet i et europeisk perspektiv. Oslo: NOVA-rapport 7-2004 (Families, welfare states, and ageing. Family solidarity in a European perspective).

Daatland, S.O., & Lowenstein, A. (2005). Intergenerational solidarity and family-welfare state balance. *European Journal of Ageing*, 2. pp. 174-182.

Das, T.H. (1983). Qualitative research in organizational behaviours. *Journal of Management Studies*, 3, 301-314.

Davis, F. (1971). *On Youth Subcultures: The Hippie Variant*. New York: General Learning Press.

Davis, K. (1940). The sociology of parent-youth conflict. *American Sociological Review*, 5, 523-535.

Dean, A., Kolodny, B., & Wood, P. (1990) Effect of social support from various sources on depression on elderly persons. *Journal of Health and Social Behaviour*, 31, 48-61.

Dekovic, M. (1999). Parent adolescent conflict: Possible determinants and consequences. *Journal of Behavioural Development*, Vol. 23, No. 4, 1, 977-1000 (24).

Dekovic, M. Pels, T., & Model, S. (2006).*Unity and Diversity in Child Rearing: Family Life in Multicultural Society*, Lewiston, NY: Edwin Mellen Press.

Deutsch, M. (1975). Equity, equality, and need: What determines which value will be used as the basis of distributive justice? *Journal of Social Issues, 31*, 137–149.

Dhurvarajan, V. (1988). Religious ideology and interpersonal relationships within the family. *Journal of Comparative Family Studies, 19*, 273–285.

Diaz-Guerrero, R.C. (1967). Socio-cultural premise, attitude and cross-cultural research. *International Journal of Psychology*, 2, 79-87.

Diener, E. & Such, E.M. (1998). Subjective well-being and age: An International Analysis. In K.W. Schaie & M.P. Lawton (Eds.) *Annual Review of Gerontology and Geriatrics* (Vol.17, pp. 304-324). New York: Press.

Diener, E. & Diener, C. (1996). Most People are Happy. *Psychological Science,* 7:181-85.

Diener, E. Lucas, R.E. & Oishi (2002). Subjective well-being "The Science of Happiness and Life Satisfaction". In Snyder, C. R. and Lopez, S.J. (Eds.) *Handbook of Positive Psychology*. Oxford University Press, New York.

Dixit, R.C. & Moorjani, J.D. (1981). *Self-Concepts and Level of aspiration as related to the socio-economic backwardness among young children.* Psychalingua.

Dowd, J.J. (1980). *Stratification Among the Aged.* Monterey, CA: Brooks/ Cole.

Dressel, P.L., & Clark, A. (1990). A critical look at family care. *Journal of Marriage and Family,* 52, 769-782.

Drury, L., Hutchison, P., & Abrams, D. (2016). Direct and extended intergenerational contact and young people's attitudes towards older adults. *British Journal of Social Psychology, 55*(3), 522-543. http://dx.doi.org/10.1111/bjso.12146

Dunham, C.C. (1995) A link between generations: Intergenerational relations and aging parents. *Journal of Family Issues.*16, 450-465.

Durkheim, E. (1928). Contemporary Sociological Theories, in, Jeffrey C. Alexander, Philip Smith (eds.) *The Cambridge Companion to Durkheim,* Combridge: Cambridge University Press.

Durkheim, E. (1964). *The Division of Labour in Society*. Free Press, New York.

Eisenstadt, S.N. (1956). *From Generation to Generation.* Glencoe Ill. The Free Press.

Epstein, A. (1928). The Challenged of the Aged. New York: Macy-Masius, Vanguard Press.

European Journal of Ageing, 2, pp. 174-182.

Feldman, S. S. & Rosenthal, D. A. (1990).The acculturation of autonomy expectations in Chinese high-schoolers residing in two Western nations. *International Journal of Psychology,* 16, 259-281.

Fengler, A. & Jenson, L. (1981). Perceived and objective condition as a predictor of life satisfaction in urban and rural elderly, *Journal of Gerontology,* 36 (6), 750-752.

Fengler, A. & Wood, V. (1972). The generation gap: An analysis of attitudes on contemporary issues. *The Gerontologist,* 12 (2), 124-128.

Fiske, G.O. (1995). Gender hierarchy: Is it a useful concept describing family structure? In J. Van Lawick and M. Sanders (Eds.) *Family Gender and Beyond,* pp. 63-72. Heemstede, The Netherlands: L.S. Books.

Flacks, R. (1967). The liberated generation: An exploration of the roots of social protest. *Journal of Social Issues, 23,* 52-75.

Freeman, C. (1961). Economic status and adoption of new agricultural and home practices. In R.N. Saxena (Ed.) *Sociology, Social Research and Social Problems in India.* Bombay: Asia Publishing House.

Fuligni, A. J. (1998). The adjustment of children from immigrant families. Current direction in *Psychological Science,* 7, 99-103.

Fuligni, A. J.; Tseng, V. & Lam, M. (1999). Attitudes towards family obligations among American adolescents from Asian, American, Latin American and European background. *Child Development,* 70, 1030-1044.

Fuligni, A.J. & Pedersen, S. (2002). Family obligations and the transition to young adulthood. *Developmental Psychology,* 38, 856-868.

Fuligni, A.J. (1998). At the adjustment of children from immigrants families. Current direction in *Psychological Science,* 7, 99-103.

Gangrade, K.D. (1975). *Crisis of Values: A Study of Intergeneration Gap.* Chetna Publications, New Delhi.

George, L.K. (1986). Caregiver burden: Conflict between norms reciprocity and solidarity. In K. Pillmer and R. Wolf (Eds.) *Elder Abuse Conflict in the Family* (pp. 67-92). Dover, M.A.: Auburn House. *Gerontologist,* 11, 90–101.

Gim Chung, R.H. (2001). Gender, ethnicity and acculturation in intergenerational conflict of Asian American college students. *Cultural Diversity and Ethnic Minority Psy*chology, 7, 376-386.

Glenn, N.D. (1977). *Cohort Analysis.* Sage Publications. Beverly Hills, California.

Gold, S.J. (1989). Differential adjustment among immigrant family members. *Journal of Contemporary Ethnography,* 17, 408-434.

Goldstein, M., Schuler, S. & Ross, J.L. (1983). Social and economic forces affecting intergenerational relations in extended family in a third world country: A cautionary tale from South Asia, *Journal of Gerontology,* 38 (6), 716-724.

Gordner, M. (1981). *Caring and Sharing Perspective on Aging,* X (January-Feb), 4-7.

Gore, M.S. (1965). The Traditional Indian Family. In M.F. Nimkoff (eds.) *Comparative Family Systems.* Boston: Houghton Mifflin.

Gore, M.S. (1968). *Urbanization and Family Change.* Bombay: Popular Prakashan.

Green, S. K. (1981). Attitudes and perceptions about the elderly: Current and future perspectives. *International Journal of Aging and Human Development,* 13, 99–119.

Greenberger, E. & Chen, C. (1996). Perceived family relationship and depressed mood in early and late adolescence: A compression of European and Asian Americans. *Developmental Psychology,* 32, 707-716.

Greene, R.W. & Feld, S. (1989) Social support coverage and the well-being of elderly widows and married women. *Journal of Family Issues*,10,33-51.

Gulati, L. (1983). "Male Migration to the Middle-East and the Impact on the Family Some Evidences from Kerala." *Economic and Political Weekly*. XVIII. Nos. 52 & 53 (December 24-31).

Hall, G. S. (1922). *Senescence, the Second Half of Life.* New York: Appleton.

Hall, N.R., Hart, D. & Mitlin, D. (Eds.) (1996).*The Urban Opportunity.* London: Intermediate Technology Publication.

Hasting, D.W. and Berry, L. (1979). Introduction: An Overview of Cohort Analysis. In: Hasting, D.W. and L. Berry (eds.), *Cohort Analysis: A Collection of Interdisciplinary Readings*, Oxford: Scripps Foundations.

Heslop, A. (1995). Assessment into the needs of older people in Mobodhonwa, Northern.

Hill, R. (1970b). The three generation research design: Method for studying family and social change. In R. Hill & R. Konig (Eds.), *Families in East and West: Socialization Process and Kinship Ties.* Paris: Moulton.

Hill, R., Foote, N., Aldous, J., Carlson, R., & MacDonald, R. (1970). *Family Development in Three Generations.* Cambridge, MA: Schenkman.

Ho, M.K. (1987). *Family Therapy with Ethnic Minorities.* Newbury Park, CA: Sage.

Homans, G. (1958). Social behaviour as exchange. *American Journal of Sociology*, 42, 597-606.

Ishie-Kuntz, M. (1997). Intergenerational relationship among Chinese, Japanese and Korean American. *Family Relations*, 46, 23-32.

Jennings, M. K. & Niemi, R. G. (1968). The transmission of political values from parent to child. *American Political Science Review*, 42, 169-184.

Kagtcibasi, C. (1982). *The Changing Values of Children in Turkey, Honolulu, Hawaii*: East-West Center, Publ. No. 60-E.

Kagtcibasi, C. (1982b). *The Changing Values of Children in Turkey, Honolulu, Hawaii*: East-West Center, Publ.No.60-E.

Kagtcibasi, C. (2002). A model of family change in cultural context. In W.J. Lonner, D.L. Dinnel, S.A. Hayes and D.N. Sattler (Eds.) *Online Readings in Psychology and Culture (Unit 13, Chapter, 1).* Retrieved from://www.wwu.edu/culture.

Kandel, D. (1974). Inter- and intra-generational influences on adolescent marijunause. *Journal of Social Issues*, 30(2).

Kasschau, P.L., Ransford, H.E., & Bengtson, V.L. (1974). Generational consciousness and youth movement participation: Contrasts in blue collar and white collar youth. *Journal of Social Issues*, 30(3).

Katz, R. & Lowenstein, A. (1999). Adjustment of older soviet immigrant's parents and their children residing is shared households: an Intergenerational Compression, *Family Relations*, 48 (1): 45-50.

Keating, N. & Marshall, J. (1980). The process of retirement: The rural self-employed, *The Gerontologist*, 20 (4), 437-443.

Kelly, S.J., Whitley, D., Spie, T.A. & Yorker, B.C. (2001). Psychological distress in grandmothers' kinship care providers: The role of resources, social support and physical health. *Child Abuse & Neglect*, 24, 311-321.

Keniston, K. (1968). *Yong radicals.* New York: Harcourt, Brace & World.

Kessler, C.R., McReod, D.J. & Wethington, E. (1985). The costs of aging: A perspective on the relationship between sex and psychological distress. In I. Sarason & B. Sarason (Eds.), *Social Support, Theory, Research, and Applications*, (pp. 491-506). The Hague: Martinus Nijhoff.

Khatri, A.A. (1975). The adaptive extended family in India today. *Journal of Marriage and Family, 37*: 633-647.

Kim, P. & Wilson, C. (1981).*Towards Mental Health of Rural Elderly.* Lanham, Md: University Press of America.

Kitagwa, E.M. & Hauser, P.M. (1973). *Differential Mortality in the United States.* Cambridge: Harvard University Press.

Kite, M.E., & Johnson, B. T. (1988). Attitudes toward older and younger adults: A meta-analysis. *Psychology and Aging*, 3, 233–244.

Kohn, M.L. (1963). Social class and parent child relationship and interpretation, *American Journal of Sociology*, 68 (4), 471-480.

Kohn, M.L. (1969). *Class and Conformity: Study in Values.* Illinois: The Dorsey Press.

Komter, A.E. & Vollebergh, W.A.M. (2002). Solidarity in Dutch families: Families ties under strain. *Journal of Family Issues, 27*, 171-188.

Koutrelakos, J. (2004). Acculturation of Greek Americans: Change and continuity in cognitive schema guiding intimate relationship. *International Journal of Psychology, 39*, 95-105.

Krause, N. (1987). Chronic financial strain, social support, and depressive symptoms among older adults. *Psychology and Aging*, 2:185-92.

Kruase, N., Liang, J., & Keith, V. (1990) Personality, social support, and psychological distress in later life. *Psychology and Aging*, 5, 315-326.

Krause, N., Herzog, R.A., & Baker, E. (1992). Providing support to others and well-being in later life. *Journal of Gerontology: Psychological Science*, 47, 300-311.

Kuppuswamy, B. (1962). *Socio-Economic Status Scale (Urban).* Delhi: Manasayan.

Kwak, K. (2003). Adolescents and their parents: A review of intergenerational family relations for immigrants and non-immigrants. *Human Development, 46*, 115-136.

La Rossa, R. & Wolf, J.H. (1985). On qualitative family research. *Journal of Marriage and Family, 47*, 531-542.

Labov, W. & Waletzky, J. (1967). Narrative analysis: oral version of personal experience. In J. Helm (Ed.), *Essays on the Verbal and Visual Arts.* Seattle: University of Washington Press. pp.12-44.

Lacy, W. & Hendricks, J. (1980). Development models of adult life: Myth and reality. *International Journal of Aging and Human Development*, 11 (2), 89-110.

Lalaycioglu, S. & Tilic, R.H. (2000). Intergenerational solidarity network of instrumental and cultural transfers within migrant families in Turkey. *Aging and Society*, 20, 223-242.

Landis, J. (1940). *Attitude and Adjustment of Aged Rural People in Iowa.* Ph.D. Thesis, Louisiana State University.

Laufer, R.S. & Bengtson, V.L. (1974). Generations, aging and social stratification on the development of generational unit. *Journal of Social Issues*, 3 (30), 181-205.

Laursen, B. & Collins, W.A. (1994). Interpersonal conflict during adolescence. *Psychological Bulletin*, 115, 197-209.

Laursen, B. Coy, K.C. & Collins, W.A. (1998). Reconsidered changes in parent child conflict across adolescence. A Meta-Analysis. *Child Development*, 69, 817-832.

Lazarus, R.S. & Folkman, S. (1984). *Stress: Appraisal and Coping*. New York: Springer.

Lee, G.R. & Ellithorpe, E. (1982). Intergenerational exchange and subjective well-being among the elderly. *Journal of Marriage and Family*, 44, 217-24.

Lee, G.R., Netzer, J.K. & Coward, R.T. (1995). Depression among older parents: The role of intergenerational assistance. *Journal of Marriage and the Family*, 56, 559-565.

Lee, G.R; & Ishi-Kuntz, M. (1987). Social Interaction, Loneliness and Emotional Well-being among the Elderly, *Research on Aging*, 9, pp. 459-482.

Lee, J. & Cynn, V. (1991). Issues in counselling 1.5 generations Korean American. In C. Lee & B. Richardson (Eds.) *Multicultural Issues in Counselling New Approach to Diversity* (pp. 127-140). Alexandria, VA: American Association for Counselling and Development.

Lee, R.M., Choe, J., Kim, G. & Nago, V. (2000). Construction of Asian American family conflicts scale. *Journal of Counselling Psychology*, 47, 211-222.

Lee, R., M. & Liu, H.,T.T. (2001). Coping with intergenerational conflict: Comparisons of Asian American, Hispanic and European-American college student. *Journal of Counselling Psychology*, 48,410-419.

Legros, B.B. (2002). Introduction-filiations and identity: Towards a sociology of intergenerational relations. *Current Sociology*, March 2002, 50(2), 175-183.

Leitch, T. (1986).*What Stories Are: Narrative Theory and Interpretation*. USA: Pennsylvania State University.

Lendon, J. (2017). A Decade of Love and Hate. *Journal of Family Issues*, *38*(3), 336-357.

Lennartsson, C., Silverstein, M. & Fritzell, J. (2010). Time-for-money exchanges between older and younger generations in Swedish families, *Journal of Family Issues, 31*, 189-210.

Lewis, O. & Dhillon, H.S. (1955). *Leadership and Groups in a South Indian Village*. Delhi: P.E.O. Publications No. 9.

Lieblich, A., Tuval-Maschiach, R. & Zilber, T. (1998). *Narrative Research: Reading, Analysis, and Interpretation*. Thousand Oaks, CA: Sage.

Lin, K.M. (1986). Psychopathology and social disruption in refuges. In C.L. Williams and Westermeyer (Eds.) *Refugee Mental Health in Resettlement Countries* (pp. 61-71). Washington, DC: Hemisphere.

Linton, R. (1942). Age and sex categories. *American Sociological Review, 7 (5)*, 589-603.

Lowenstein, A. (2002). Solidarity and conflict in co-residence of three generational immigrant families from Soviet Union. *Journal of Aging Studies, 16*, 221-241.

Lowenstein, A., Katz, R., Daatland, S.V., & Bazo, M.T. (2001). *Family norms and practices in a comparative perspective*. Paper presented at the International Symposium on International Perspective on Families, Aging and Social Support, Haifa.

Lowenstein, A., Katz, R., & Guryaish, N. (2007). Reciprocity in parent-child exchange and life satisfaction among the elderly: A cross national perspective. *Journal of Social Issues, 63*, 865-884.

Lüscher, K. (1998). *A heuristic model for the study of intergenerational ambivalence*. Working paper# 29. Germany: University at Fonstanz. Research Center Society.

Lüscher, K. (2010). Homo ambivalens. *Psychotherapeut, 54*, 136–146.

Lüscher, K. (2011). Ambivalence: A "Sensitizing Construct" for the study and practice of intergenerational relationships, *Journal of Intergenerational Relationships*, 9, 191–206.

Lüscher, K. & Pillmer, K. (1998). Intergenerational ambivalence: A new approach to study of parent-child relation in later life. *Journal of Marriage and Family*, 60, 413-425.

Magnusson, D. & Torested, B. (1993). A holistic view of personality: A model revisited. *Journal of Personality and Social Psychology*, 35, 63-78.

Mahne, K. & Kingebiel, A.M. (2012). The importance of the grandparent role—A class specific phenomenon? Evidence from Germany. *Advances in Life Course Research*, 17, 145–155.

Mandelbaum, D.G. (1959). The family in India. In R.N. Anshen (ed.) *The Family: Its Function and Destiny* (p. 167). New York: Harper.

Mannheim, K. (1952). *The Problem of Generation in Essays in the Sociology of Knowledge*. London: Routledge & Kegan Paul.

Mannheim, K. (1972). "The Problem of Generations." In Philip G. Altbach and Robert S. Laufer (eds.), *The New Pilgrims*. New York: David McKay (originally published in 1928).

Marshall, V. W., Matthews, S. H. & Rosenthal, C.J. (1993). Elusiveness of family life: A challenge for the sociology of aging. In G.L. Maddox and M. Powell Lawton (Eds.), *Annual Review of Gerontology and Geriatrics: Focus on Kinship Aging and Social Change* (pp. 39-72). New York: Springer.

Martin, L.G. (1990a). Changing intergenerational family relations in East Asia. *The Annals*, No. 510 (July), pp. 102-114.

Martin, W. (1986). *Recent Theories of Narrative*. Ithaca, NY: Cornell University Press.

Maslow, A.H. (1970). *Motivation and Personality*. New York: Harper & Row.

Mason, K.P. (1991). Family change and Support of the elderly in Asia: What do we Know? Paper presented in at the joint ESCAP/ JOICFP workshop on Population Aging in Asia, Bangkok, 15-22 July.

McPherson (1983). *Aging as a Social Process*. Butterworth & Co., Canada.

McTavish, D.G. (1971). Perceptions of old people: *A Review of Research Methodologies and Findings*.

Medley, M.L. (1980). Life satisfaction across four stages of adult life. *International Journal of Aging and Human Development*, 11, 193-209.

Mednick, S., Harway, M. & Finello, K. (1984). *Handbook of Longitudinal Research*. New York: Praeger.

Medora, N.P. (2008). Strengths and challenges in the Indian family. *Marriage & Family Review*, 41,165-193.

Mena, F.J., Padilla, A.M. & Maldonado (1987). Acculturative stress and specific coping strategies among immigrant and later generation college student. *Hispanic Journal of Behavioural Science*, 9, 207-225.

Merton, R.K. & Barber, E. (1963). Sociological ambivalence. In E. Triyakin (Eds.) *Sociological Theory: Values and Sociocultural Change* (pp. 91-120). New York: Howorth.

Merz, E.M. (2005). *Transgressing Borders between Sociology and Psychology: A Case of Intergenerational Solidarity*. Frontiers of Sociology, Stockholm Sweden, July 5-9, 2005. *info.hs@scasss.vv.se*.

Merz, E.M., Schuengel, C. & Schulze, H.J. (2007). Intergenerational solidarity: An attachment perspective. *Journal of Aging Studies*.Vol.21, (2), 175-186.

Min, J., Silverstein, M., & Lendon, J.P. (2012). Intergenerational transmission of values over the family life course. *Advances in Life Course Research* 17 (2012): 112–120.

Min, P. (1998).The Korean American family. In C. Mindel, R. Habenstein & R. Wright (Eds.) *Ethnic Families in Americas: Pattern and Variations* (pp. 191-229). Englewood Cliffs, NJ: Prentice Hall.

Mishler, E. G. (1995). Models of narrative analysis: A typology. *Journal of Narrative and Life History, 5 (2)*, 87-123.

Mishra, G. & Prasad, D. (1978). A study of meaning differences across generations in India. *Indian Journal of Applied Psychology*, 13 (1), 6-10.

Mishra, R.C., & Tiwari, B.B. (1980). Intergenerational attitudes: A psychological analysis. *Psychologia: An International Journal of Psychology in the Orient*. Vol. 23(3) Oct. 1980, 160-166.

Mittness, L. S. (1990). Knowledge and beliefs about urinary incontinence in adulthood and old age. *Journal of the American Geriatric Society*, 38, 374-378.

Morgan, G. & Simrcich (1980). *The Case for Qualitative Research: Academy of Management Review*, (4), 491-500.

Moss, M. S. and Moss, S.Z. (1992). Themes and parent child relationship when the elderly parent move nearby. *Journal of Aging Studies*, 6, 259-271.

N.R., Hart, D. & Mitlin, D. (Eds.) (1996). *The Urban Opportunity*. London: Intermediate Technology Publication.

Naidu, U.S. (1981). Self-image of Schedule Caste educated youth. *Indian Journal of Social Work*. XLII (2), 149-154. New Delhi.

Newgarten, V. (1979).The middle generations (pp. 258-66). In P. Ragan (Eds.) *Aging Parents*. Los Angeles: University of Southern California.

Non, S., Beiser, M., Kaspar, V. Hov, F. & Rummens, J. (1999). Perceived racial discrimination, depression and coping: A study of South-East Asian Refugees in Canada. *Journal of Health and Social Behaviour*, 40, 193-207.

O'Brien, M., Margalin, G., & John, R.S. (1995). Relation among marital conflict, child coping and child adjustment. *Journal of Clinical Child Psychology*, 24, 346-361.

Orum, A. (1972). Introduction: Perspective on youth and politics in America. In A. Orum (Ed.), *The Seeds of Politics: Youth and Politics in America*. Englewood Cliffs, N.J.: Prentice-Hall.

Padilla, J., McHale, S., Rovine, M., Updegraff, K., & Umaña-Taylor, A. (2016). Parent-Youth Differences in Familism Values from Adolescence into Young Adulthood: Developmental Course and Links with Parent-Youth Conflict. *Journal of Youth and Adolescence, 45*(12), 2417-2430.

Palmore, E.B. (1981a). More on Palmore's Facts on Aging Quiz. *Gerontologist*, 21, 115–116.

Panda, A.K. (2004). Grandmothers: Needed or avoided? *Indian Journal of Gerontology*, 18 (3 & 4).

Pandey, J. (2007). Family in India in J. Georgas, J. Berry, C. Kazatabasi, & Y.H. Poortinga, (Eds.) *Family Across Thirty Cultures*, Cambridge Press.

Parsons, T. (1942). Age and sex in the social structure of the United States. *American Sociological Review*, 7 (5), 604-620.

Pavot, W. & Diener, E. (1993). Review of the Satisfaction with Life Scale. *Psychological Assessment*, 5:164-72.

Penning, M.J. & Strain, L.A. (1994) Gender difference in disability, assistance and subjective well-being in later life. *Journal of Gerontology: Social Science*, 49, 202-208.

Pfeffer, J. (1990). Management as a symbolic action: The correlation and maintenance of organizational paradigms. In L.L. Cummings and

B.M. Staw (Eds.), *Information and Cognition in Organization.* Greenwhich, CT: JAI.

Phalet, K. & Schonpflug, U. (2001). Intergenerational transmission of collectivism and achievement values in two acculturation context: The case of Turkish families in Germany and Turkis and Moroccan families in Netherlands. *Journal of Cross Cultural Psychology,* 32,186-201.

Phinney, J.S., Ong, A. & Madden, T. (2000). Cultural value and intergenerational value discrepancies in immigrants and non-immigrants families. *Child Development,* 71, 528-539.

Pillemer, K. & Lüscher, K. (Eds.) (2004). *Intergenerational ambivalence: New perspective on parent-child relations in later life.* Stamford, CT: Elsevier/JAI Press.

Pillemer, K. & Suitor, J.J. (2002). Explaining mothers' ambivalence towards adult children. *Journal of Marriage & the Family,* 65, 602-613.

Pillemer, K. & Suitor, J.J. (2005). Ambivalence in intergenerational relations over the life-course. In M. Silverstein, R. Giarrusso & V.L. Bengtson (Eds.), *Intergenerational Relations Across Time and Place* (pp 3-28). New York: Springer.

Pillemer, K., Suitor, J.J., Mock, S.E., Sabir, M., Pardo, T.B., & Sechrist, J. (2007). Capturing the complexity of intergenerational relations: Exploring ambivalence within later-life families. *Journal of Social Issues,* 63 (4), 775-791.

Pitts, J.R. (1969). The Hippies as a contra-meritocracy. *Dissent,* 326-337.

Prakash, I.J. (1996). Intergenerational differences in attitude towards women. *Indian Journal of Gerontology.* 10 (1& 4), 34-38. *Psychologia—An International Journal of Psychology in the Orient.* Vol. XXIII, No.3 October.

Qvortrup, J. (2000). A childhood perspective applied to Wolfgang Lutz's paper. In *Tranka.* 70. 73.

Ragan, P.K. & Dowd, J. J. (1974). Emerging political consciousness of the aged: A generational interpretation. *Journal of Social Issues,* 30(3).

Raju, S.S. (2002). Meeting the needs of the older poor and excluded in India, situation and voices: The older poor and excluded in South Africa and India, *UNFPA Population and Development Strategies,* No.2, 93-110.

Rammurthi, P.V. (2002). Intergenerational Relations. In K.R. Gangadharan (Eds.) *Aging in India: Emerging Trends and Perspective,* Heritage Hospital, Hyderabad, 24-26.

Rank, M. R. (1992). The blending of qualitative and quantitative methods. In J.F. Gulgen; K. Daily and G. Handel (Eds.), *Qualitative Methods in Family Research* (pp. 281-322), Newbury Park: Sage Publications.

Rath, R. (1971). Generation gap as a psychological factor of social change. Proceeding of 38th session of Indian Science Congress.

Rawat, P.S., and Rawat, K. (1986). "Rural-Urban migration: Impact on the villages." *The Eastern Anthropologist.* 39 (2), 115 -124.

Riessman, C.K. (1990). *Divorce Talk.* New Brunswick, NJ: Rutgers University Press

Rikhye, K. & Chaddha, N.K. (1998). Intergeneration gaps and its consequences in old age. *Aging and Society,* Vol.8, No. 3 & 4, 57-72.

Riley, M. W., Johnson, M., & Foner, A. (1972). *Aging and Society: A Sociology of Age Stratification* (Vol. 3). New York: Russell Sage Foundation.

Roberts, R.E.L. & Bengtson, V. L. (1991). Intergenerational Solidarity a unidimensional construct? A second test of formal model, *Journal of Gerontology: Social Science,* 45: 512-520.

Roberts, R.E.L., Richards, L.N., & Bengtson, V. L. (1991). Intergenerational solidarity in families: Untangling the ties that bind. In S.K. Pfeifer & M.B. Sussman (Eds.*). Marriage and Family Review,* Vol. 16. Haworth Press, Binghamton, NY: 11-46.

Rokeach, M. (1973). *The Nature of Human Values.* New York: Free Press.

Rosenberg, M. (1965). *Society and the Adolescent Self-image.* Prinston: Prinston University Press.

Rossi, A. S. & Rossi, P. H. (1990). *Of Human Bonding: Parent-child Relations Across the Life Course.* New York: Aldine de Greyter.

Ruiz, S.A. & Silverstein, M. (2007). Relationship with Grandparents and the Emotional well-being of Late Adolescent and Young Grandchildren. *Journal of Social Issues,* 63,827-844.

Russell, D. W., & Cutrona, C. (1991). Social support stress and depressive symptoms among the elderly: Test of process model. *Psychology and Aging,* 6, 190-201.

Ryder, N. (1965). The cohort as a concept in the study of social change. *American Sociological Review.*

Santos, J.D. & Levitt, M.J. (2007). Intergenerational relations with in-laws in the context of the social convey: Theoretical and Practical implication. *Journal of Social Issues,* 63: 827-844.

Schaie, K. (1965). A general model for the study of developmental problems. *Psychological Bulletin,* 64; 92-107.

Schenk, N. & Dkstra, P.A. (2012). Continuity and change in Intergenerational family relationships: An examination of shifts in relationship type over a three-year period. *Advances in Life Course Research,* 17 (2012): 121-132.

Seelbach, W.C. & Die, A. (1988). Family satisfaction and filial norms among Vietnamese immigrants. *Journal of Aging Studies,* 2, 267-276.

Sen, K. (1994). *Aging: Database on Demographic Transition and Social Policy.* London: Zed Books.

Shans, E. (1967). Family help pattern and social class in three countries. *Journal of Marriage and Family,* 29 (2), 257-266.

Sharma, G.C & Tiwari, G. (1983). Gerontology: Viewpoint of Hindu Psychology. *Perspective in Psychological Research,* 6(1), 19-24.

Sharma, S. (1999). Social Support, Stress and Psychological Well-being. In G. Mishra (eds.) *Psychological Perspective on Stress and Health* (pp.126-146) New Delhi: Concept Publishing Company.

Sherif, M. & Sherif, E.W. (1953). *Group in Harmony and Tension: An Integration of Studies on Inter-group Relations*, New York: Octagon.

Shumaker, S., & Brownell, A. (1984) Toward a theory of social support: closing conceptual gaps. *Journal of Social Issues*, 40, 11-36.

Silverstein, M., & Bengtson, V.L. (1994). Does intergenerational support influence the psychological well-being of older parents? The contingencies of dealing health and widowhood. *Social Science and Medicine*, 38(7), 943-957.

Silverstein, M., & Lendon, J.P. (2012). Intergenerational transmission of values over the family life course. *Advances in Life Course Research*, 17 (3): 112-120.

Simmel, G. (1950). *The Sociology of George Simmel*. Glencoe ILL: Free Press.

Singh, S. & Chaddha, N.K. (2004). *Intergenerational Relationship Study of Life Satisfaction, Attitude Role and Expectation*. Unpublished project report. Department of Psychology, University of Delhi, Delhi.

Sinha, D. (1969). *Indian Villages in Transition: A Motivational Analysis*. New Delhi: Associational Publishing House.

Sinha, D. (1972). *The Mughal Syndrome. A Psychological Study of Intergenerational Differences*. Bombay-New Delhi: Tata McGraw-Hill Publishing Co. Ltd.

Sinha, D. (1984). Some recent changes in the Indian family and their implications for socialization. *Indian Journal of Social Work*, 45,271-286.

Skinner, E.A., Edge, K., Altman, J., & Sherwood, H. (2003). Searching for the structure of coping: A review and critique of category system for classifying ways of coping. *Psychological Bulletin*, 129, 216-269.

Slater, P. (1970). *The Pursuit of Loneliness*. Boston: Beacon Press.

Sluzki, C. (1979) Migration and Family Conflict. *Family Process*, 18, 379-390. *Socialization*: *Indian Journal of Social Work*, *45*, 271-286.

Soloman, F. (1964). Youth and Peace: A Psychological study of student Peace Demonstrators in Washington, D.C. *Journal of Social Issues*, *20(4)*, 54-73.

Somerfield, M.R. (1997). The utility of system model stress and coping for applied research. *Journal of Health Psychology*, 2,133-151.

Sonar, G.B. & Prasad, R.S. (2004). Intergenerational issues in old age: A study of Gulbarga district of Karnataka. *Indian Journal of Gerontology*, 8: 3& 4.

Spicer, J. (1997). Who and what health Psychologist talking about. Okoroire, New Zealand Fourth Health Psychology Conference.

Starr, J.M. (1974). The Peace and Love Generation: Changing attitudes towards Sex and Violence among college youth. *Journal of Social Issues*, 30(2).

Steinbach, A. (2012). Intergenerational relations across the life course. *Advances in Life Course Research*, 17 (2012) 93-99.

Steinman, L. (1979). Reactivated conflicts with aging parents (pp. 126-143). In P. Ragan (Ed.) *Aging Parents*. Los Angeles: University of Southern California Press.

Suri, S. & Chaddha, N.K. (2003) Intergenerational-Interplay of Relationships. Unpublished project report. Department of Psychology, University of Delhi, Delhi.

Syme, S.L. & Berkman, L.F. (1976). Social class, susceptibility and sickness. *American Journal of Epidemiology*, 104,1-8.

Szydlik, M. (2012). Generations: Connections across the life course. *Advances in Life Course Research*, 17 (2012): 100-111.

Tajfel, H., & Turner, J. (1979). An integrative theory of inter-group conflict. In W. Austin, & S. Worchel (Eds.), *Psychology of Inter-group Relations* (pp. 33 – 48). Monterey, CA: Brooks/Cole.

Taniguchi, H., & Kaufman, G. (2017). Filial Norms, Co-Residence, and Intergenerational Exchange in Japan. *Social Science Quarterly*. *http://dx.doi.org/10.1111/ssqu.12365*

Thibaut, J.W., and Kelley, H.H. (1959).*The Social Psychology of Groups*. New York: Wiley.

Thoists, P. (1995). Stress, coping and social support process. Where we are? What next? *Journal of Social Behaviours*, 42, 115-131.

Thomas, L.E. (1971). Political attitude congruence between politically active parents and college-age children. *Journal of Marriage and Family*, 33, 375-386.

Thomas, L. E. (1974). Generational discontinuity in beliefs: An exploration of the generation gap. *Journal of Social Issues*, 30(3).

Thompson, M.M. & Holmes, J.G. (1996). Ambivalence in close relationship: Conflicted cognitions as a catalyst for change. In R.M. Sorrentin and E.T. Higgins (Eds.) *Handbook of Motivation and Cognition*, Vol. 3: The Interpersonal Context (pp. 497-530). Houston, TX: The Guilford Press.

Tiwari, B.B. & Mishra, R.C. (1979). An intergenerational study of value orientation. *Journal of Psychological Research*, 23, 31-38.

Todorov, T. (1990). *Genres in Discourse*. Cambridge: Cambridge University Press.

Treas, J. & Bengtson, V.L. (1987). The family in later years. In M.B. Sussman & S.K. Steinmetz (Eds.), *Handbook of Marriage and Family* (pp. 625-648), New York: Plenum.

Tripathi, R.C. (1987). Applied social psychology (p. 99). In J. Pandey (Eds.) *Psychology in India: State of the Art*, Vol. 2. Sage Publications, India.

Troll, L. & Bengston, V. (1979). Generations in the family (pp. 127-161). In W. Burr, *et al.*, (Eds.) *Contemporary Theories About Family*. New York: The Free Press.

Troll, L. (1970). The generation gap: conceptual models. *Aging Human Development*, 1, 78-89.

Troll, L. (1980). Intergenerational relations in later life: A family system approach. In N. Daian & N. Lohmann (Eds.), *Transition of Aging* (pp. 75-91). New York: Academic Press.

Troll, L., Neugarten, B. L., & Kraines, R. J. (1969). Similarities in values and other personality characteristics in college student and their parents. *Merrill, Palmer Quarterly*, 15, 323-336.

Uba, L.C. (1994). *Asian American Personality Pattern Identity and Mental Health*. New York: Guilford Press.

Veenhoven, R. (1991). Is Happiness Relative. *Social Indicators Research*, 24 pp. 1-34.

Veenhoven, R. and Ehrhardt, J. (1995). The Cross-National Pattern of Happiness: Test of Predictions Implied in Three Theories of Happiness. *Social Indicators Research*, 34, pp. 33-68.

Venkatraman, M.M. (1995). "A Cross-Cultural Study of the Subjective Well-Being of Married Elderly Persons in the United States and India," *The Journals of Gerontology Series B: Psychological Sciences and Social Sciences* 50B, no. 1, S35-44.

Vera Sanso, P., (2001). Aging and intergenerational relations in urban and rural South India. Paper presented at the Development Studies Association Annual Conference, 10-12 September. Manchester: U.K.

Verma, R.M., (1962). Development of a tool to appraise socio-economic status. *Journal of Psychological Research*, 6, 35-38.

Verma, S. K. & Satayanarayana, A. (2009). A Social Psychological Study of Pattern of Intergenerational Relations: Context of Priority of Values. Unpublished manuscripts, Department of Psychology, University of Allahabad, Allahabad, Uttar Pradesh.

Verma, S.K. & Satayanarayana, A. (2012). Patterns of Intergenerational Relations in Indian Family. *Indian Journal of Gerontology*, Vol. 26, No. 3, pp. 367–385.

Vermani, S. & Sharma, M.L. (1987).Younger people's percepation of the Aged. M.L. Sharma & T.M. Dak (Eds). *Aging in India. Challenge for Society*. Ajanta Publications.

Versa-Sanso, P. (2007). Increasing consumption, decreasing support: A multi-generational study of family relations among South India Chakkliyars, *Contributions to Indian Sociology*, 41, (2): 225-248.

Vinokur, A.D. & Vinokur, K.D. (1990). "In sickness and in health": Can there be too much of a good thing ? In J.R. Greenley (Ed.), *Research in Community and Mental Health* (vol. 5). Greenwish, CT: Jai Press.

Waldrop, D.P. & Weber, J.A. (2001). From grandparent to caregiver: The stress and satisfaction of raising grandchildren. *Families in Society: The Journal of Contemporary Human Services*, 82, 461- 472.

Weigert, A J. (1991). *Mixed Emotions: Certain Steps toward Understanding Ambivalence*. Lbany: State University of New York Press.

Weisz, J.R., Rothbaum, F.M. & Blackburn, T.C. (1984). Standing out and standing in: The psychology of control in America and Japan. *American Psychologist*, 39, 955-969.

Westby, D.L. & Braungart, R. G. (1966). Class and politics in the family backgrounds of student politics activists. *American Sociological Review, 31*, 690-692.

Wieder, D.L. & Zimmerman, D.H. (1974). Generational experience and the development of freak culture. *Journal of Soçial Issues*, 30(2).

Wood, V. and Robertson, J.F. (1978). Friendship and Kinship Interaction: Differential Effect on the Morale of the Elderly, *Journal of Marriage and the Family*, 39, pp. 367-375.

Wu, L.L. (2000). Some comments on Sequence analysis and optimal matching methods in sociology: review and prospect", *Sociological Methods and Research*, 29 (1):41-64.

Yankelovich, D. (1972).*The Changing Value on Campus.* New York: Simon & Schuster.

Yen, C. & Wang, Y.W. (2000). Asian-American coping attitudes, source and practices: Implications for the indigenous counselling strategies. *Journal of College Student Development*, 41, 94-103.

Ying, Y. W., Lee, P. A., Tsai, J. L., Lee, Y. J., Tasang, M. (2001). Relationship of young adult Chilies Americans with their parents: variation by migration status and cultural orientation. *American Journal of Ortho Psychiatry*, 71, 342-349.

Youmans, E. (1963). Aging patterns in rural and urban areas of Kentucky. Lexington: University of Kentucky Agricultural Experiment Station.

Zhou, M. & Bankston, C. (1998). *Growing up American: How Vietnamese Children Adopt to Life in United States*. New York: Rusell Sage Foundation.

Index